I LIKE BIRDS

A GUIDE TO BRITAIN'S AVIAN WILDLIFE

STUART COX

Hardie Grant

QUADRILLE

Contents

Introduction

A long long time ago I was child. A slightly bird-obsessed child. Whose nose was either pointing skywards, gazing at the Kestrels that hovered over our house, or buried deep in a *Collins Bird Guide*, categorising and absorbing as much as my child-mind would hold. I was blessed to live on the edge of the South Downs, country and coast in easy reach, and to have a family that encouraged me and my brothers to take an interest in the outside world. They expanded our horizons by taking us on annual holidays to the wilds of the north of Scotland, where Golden Eagles, Eider and even Oystercatchers introduced us all to just how colourful and exotic the bird life of Britain could be. My uncle – dedicated, almost semi-pro, birdwatcher and sometime recorder for the local bird society – was always up for a challenge and would take me to see the colourful, nearly tropical, fauna of the south east whether they were Great Crested Grebes or Parakeets just beginning to establish a foothold as a naturalised bird of Britain.

But despite that upbringing I'm not a twitcher. My obsession had waned over the decades as I'd become caught up in other preoccupations of adulthood. A lifetime later I found myself settled in the north of Scotland and, separated from family by around 700 miles, began to illustrate the birds I was observing and the childhood memories they brought back. The intention was that these were purely for my Mum. But within two weeks she was diagnosed with a rare illness, succumbing to it a year later, followed in rapid succession by my father and one of my brothers. The illustrations were literally lost in a drawer.

Years later a friend opened that drawer and asked if we would "do them as cards". Myself and my partner Alison stumbled into a greeting card business, and soon fledged to become I Like Birds. Since then we've been fortunate to work with some amazing British companies, producing stationery, cards, mugs, tea pots, aprons, calendars and even eyewear. All featuring birds, all with the same intention of tapping into childhood memory, spreading our twin passions for nature and design, doing something that my mum would have been proud of.

And now? She would have been proudest of all that there's a book.

Being one part guide, one part pretty pictures, this book is a collection of illustrations and some (hopefully) interesting text about what makes each bird special. Every species of bird is unique, and every species has its own story to tell whether that be a weird evolutionary quirk, peculiar behaviour or the way that we humans have interacted – not always positively – with them over centuries. Fittingly, as so much of what I do is tied into a sense of family, my brother Stephen and uncle Chris have played a key role in coming up with facts and sprinkling some colour across the words.

The intention is that if you've never really understood all the fuss about birds then this might be a gentle introduction, told through pictures and some light reading. We've arranged it around an idea of the bird watcher's journey, starting with peering out from your kitchen window wondering "what's that bird?", and working your way out into the countryside, wilds and waters edge as the bug begins to bite. I don't expect anyone to use this as a field guide: If you're interested I'd recommend getting hold of a *Collins Bird Guide*, comprehensive in its listing of British birds, a godsend to me as a child and still my go-to as an adult out in the field. Selecting just sixty from the many hundreds of birds that frequent these islands has been difficult, so there are sure to be some personal favourites missing, but we've largely gone for personality, character and colour. Hopefully there's enough here to whet the appetite and get you out in the wilds, binoculars in one hand, field guide in the other, enjoying what's around us and revelling in our amazing biodiversity.

I hope you enjoy this book. Fingers crossed there'll be something within that'll make you go "…oh, I didn't know that". Most of all I hope it adds something, no matter how minor, to the love of birds you no doubt already have. They've been a life changer for me. I like birds. I hope you do too.

Binocular basics

Binoculars are the bird-watcher's best friend. Well, possibly. Many would argue a good bird book is more useful. But if you're semi-serious about watching birds, there's a chance that at some point you will spot one just out of sight. To save yourself from squinting, it's good to have a decent pair of 'bins' to hand.

The world of optics can get a bit confusing – and competitive. One way of spotting a serious twitcher is by taking a glance at their binoculars. Given the impression many people have of bird-watchers, you might imagine them to be non-materialistic and not too fussed by anything flashy. And that seems to hold true for almost everything – except optics. Spending upwards of a grand on a pair of bins – and maybe more on a scope – is in no way unusual. The eye-wateringly expensive models do have their advantages, but if you're a casual watcher, I wouldn't bother. You can get a good pair of bins for well under £100.

But what to look for when you buy? First, get them in your hands. You could be trudging around in all weathers with your bins wrapped around your neck for long periods, so make sure they're a comfortable weight and not too bulky.

When it comes to numbers, there are only two you really need to understand: a little one and a big one. The little one might be a 7, 8, 10, 12, or in some cases higher. That's the magnification. Get a '7' and everything will appear seven times closer and seven times bigger. If a bird is seven metres away, it will only seem a metre away through your bins. The big number is the lens size in millimetres. The bigger the lens, the more light it lets in, which means it's brighter and clearer, but also heavier. It's a trade-off between usability and portability. A bigger magnification needs a bigger lens, amplifies the mild shake of your hand, and would probably be better on a tripod. If you're going down that route, you might want to think about a scope, which is a whole different subject.

Your best bet? A pair with eight-times magnification and a 40 or 42mm lens. They'll be light enough, long enough, won't cost a fortune and, all being well, will become your twitching companion for many years.

NAKED EYE

8x   10x   15x

Beaks or bills?

Is it a beak or is it a bill? Truth is, it's either. Ducks are definitely billed and eagles definitely not, but generally the terms are interchangeable. There is no definitive definition of what makes one a beak and the other a bill. Both are parts of a bird's skull: an upper and lower mandible that's a bit like our own jaw, but extended and covered in a thin layer of skin. There is a phenomenal range of beak/bill shapes, each one finely adapted for feeding. If you want a clue to how a bird lives, look at its beak: there are probers, rippers, fine-seed pickers and cherry-stone crushers among them.

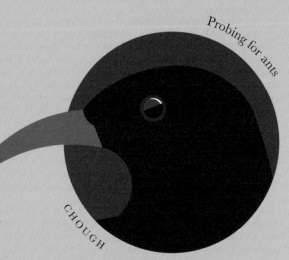

Probing for ants

CHOUGH

Sifting in shallow water

SHOVELER

Tearing and shredding

GOLDEN EAGLE

Probing for molluscs and worms

OYSTERCATCHER

Sifting deeper water

SPOONBILL

General purpose and insects

EURASIAN ROBIN

Crushing seeds and nuts

HAWFINCH

How big is a bird?

Once upon a time there were no birds, but there were definitely dinosaurs. Over millennia, these would evolve into birds. And some of them were massive. A few ancestors of these early birds co-existed with humans – the moa of New Zealand, 3.5 metres tall, survived until the 15th century when it was finally wiped out by hunters. While other big birds still exist to this day, such as the ostrich and cassowary, birds have generally become smaller over time. Many bird books are arranged by evolutionary order, with the earliest still-extant birds at the beginning and more recently evolved

types at the back, and this shows a steady move towards miniaturisation: swans and geese at the start, buntings bringing up the rear.

The largest bird you'll find in Britain is the mute swan, which is around 1.2 metres long. The smallest? The goldcrest at just nine centimetres. In between are birds of every size, colour, shape and behaviour imaginable, from short and dumpy wrens to tall and elegant cranes, plump pigeons, tiny tits, and great soaring eagles with two-metre-plus wingspans.

There are many components to identifying a bird, but putting location and behaviour to one side, two good starting points are size and shape. Birds tend to hang out together, so once you can recognise the rough size of a few species – blue tits, blackbirds, crows and herons, for example – the size of every other bird becomes relatively easy to judge. Even so, there might be some that throw you: I always imagine the great spotted woodpecker to be a lot bigger than the blackbird-sized bird it is.

ROUGH SIZES LITTLE TO LARGE

Very small	3 inches (Goldcrests) – 5 inches (Wrens)
Small	5 inches (Blue tits) – 10 inches (Blackbirds)
Medium	10 inches (Puffin) –15 inches (Sandwich tern)
Large	15 inches (Wood pigeon) – 35 inches (Golden eagle)
Very large	35+ inches (Crane and Heron)

Eggs

All birds lay eggs. It's a remnant of their 'we-used-to-be-lizards' DNA. The answer to the question, 'Which came first, the chicken or the egg?', should really be dinosaurs. However, for some reason, it's always birds that first come to mind whenever we think about eggs.

The standard colour for bird eggs is white, but many birds lay eggs of differing hues. These mainly range from blues and greens to reds and browns, all produced by a mixture of the chemical pigments biliverdin and protoporphyrin. They've developed this way for camouflage – bird eggs are a favourite snack of a wide range of animals, from foxes and squirrels to other birds, such as crows, as well as us humans. As a rule of thumb, if a bird nests in a tree or hedge, it will lay blue or green eggs; if it nests on the ground, its eggs will be a buff brownish colour. Evolution is always rational.

Some birds build nests that are tight baskets of sticks, twigs, moss, leaves and feathers. These usually have high walls, which makes keeping all their contents together fairly straightforward, so the eggs inside tend to be roundish. Meanwhile, birds that nest on the ground or cliffs, which make do with a scrape or bare rock, tend towards conical eggs. That way, any rolling eggs will normally end up going around in circles.

The clutch, or number of eggs laid in one go, varies from species to species and also from clutch to clutch, although there's a 'normal' range. Some birds, such as puffins, lay one egg, once a year. Others, such as blue tits and partridges, really go for it, laying anything up to 13 or more at a time. And while most fledglings are pretty much helpless, a partridge family is ready to run as soon as it's hatched.

Common Garden Birds

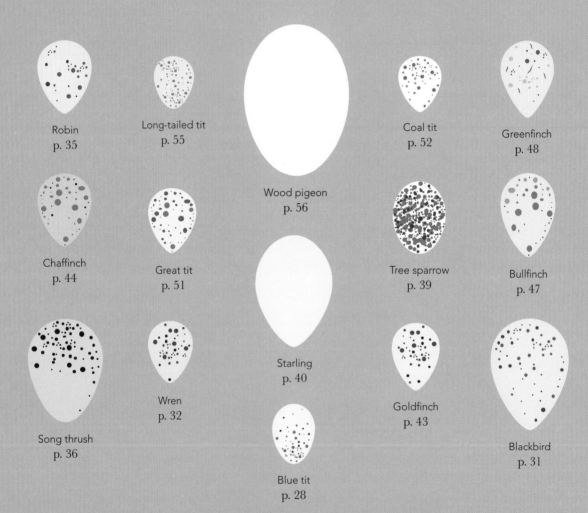

Robin
p. 35

Long-tailed tit
p. 55

Wood pigeon
p. 56

Coal tit
p. 52

Greenfinch
p. 48

Chaffinch
p. 44

Great tit
p. 51

Tree sparrow
p. 39

Bullfinch
p. 47

Song thrush
p. 36

Wren
p. 32

Starling
p. 40

Goldfinch
p. 43

Blackbird
p. 31

Blue tit
p. 28

Coast & Wetlands

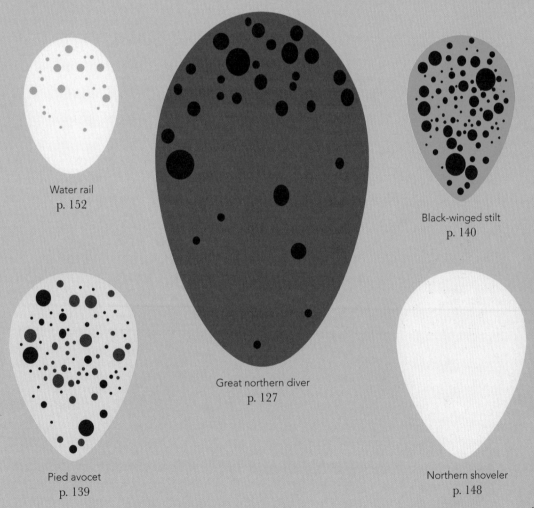

Water rail
p. 152

Black-winged stilt
p. 140

Great northern diver
p. 127

Pied avocet
p. 139

Northern shoveler
p. 148

Atlantic puffin
p. 124

Common eider
p. 132

Grey heron
p. 147

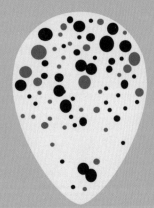

Sandwich tern
p. 135

Great crested grebe
p. 144

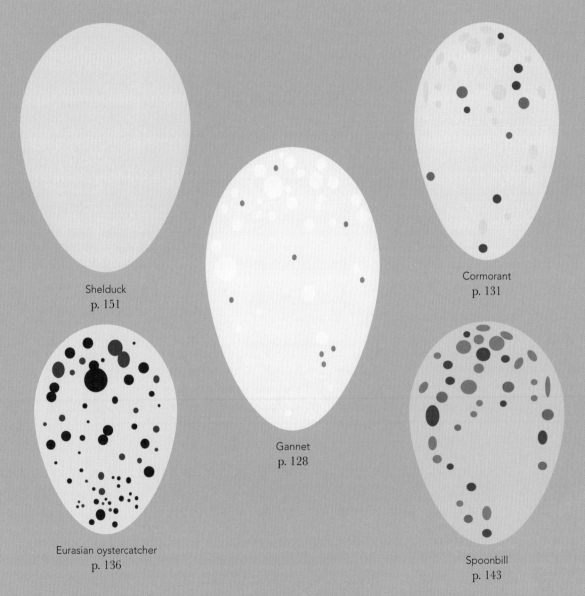

Shelduck
p. 151

Cormorant
p. 131

Gannet
p. 128

Eurasian oystercatcher
p. 136

Spoonbill
p. 143

Birds of the Countryside

Grey partridge
p. 91

Tawny owl
p. 68

Green
woodpecker
p. 75

Yellowhammer
p. 63

Redwing
p. 67

Hawfinch
p. 79

Nuthatch
p. 76

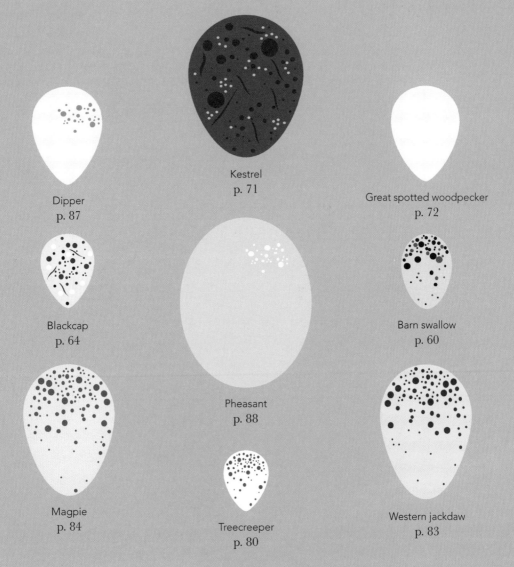

Dipper
p. 87

Kestrel
p. 71

Great spotted woodpecker
p. 72

Blackcap
p. 64

Barn swallow
p. 60

Magpie
p. 84

Pheasant
p. 88

Western jackdaw
p. 83

Treecreeper
p. 80

Birds of the Wilder Places

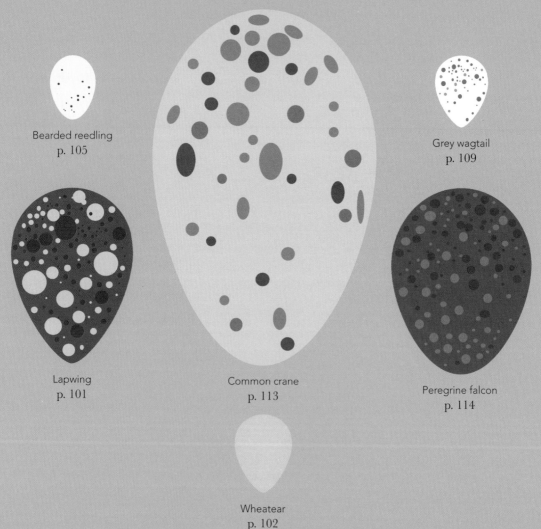

Bearded reedling
p. 105

Grey wagtail
p. 109

Lapwing
p. 101

Common crane
p. 113

Peregrine falcon
p. 114

Wheatear
p. 102

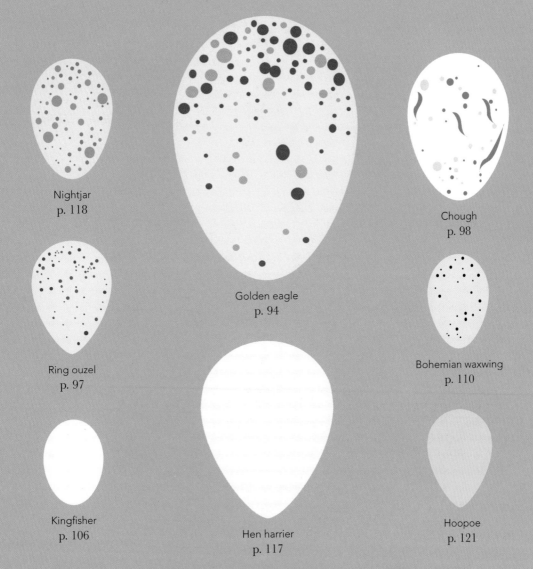

Nightjar
p. 118

Golden eagle
p. 94

Chough
p. 98

Ring ouzel
p. 97

Bohemian waxwing
p. 110

Kingfisher
p. 106

Hen harrier
p. 117

Hoopoe
p. 121

23

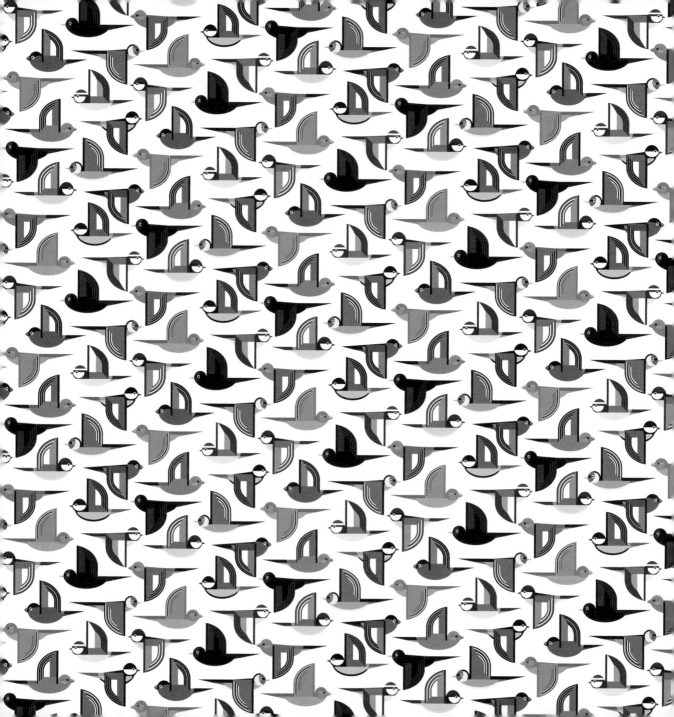

The Birds

Common Garden Birds

It doesn't take a lot to begin birdwatching. All you need is a window. Most people's first experience of watching birds is in their own garden or at a local park. Our garden birds are the most familiar but also among our most colourful and quixotic species. Being so close at hand, they give you the opportunity to observe their unique behaviours at length across the seasons. These are the birds we all know and love. And each has a story to tell.

Blue tit

Cyanistes caeruleus

FAMILY
Paridae – tits and chickadees

HABITAT
Gardens, hedges and mixed woodland

SIZE
12cm long, 18cm wingspan

DIET
Seeds, insects and spiders

BREEDS
April–May, one brood

NEST
Mossy cup, lined with feathers

EGGS
Seven to 16. White with urplish speckles

RANGE
Found across the UK

COLLECTIVE NOUN
Banditry

OLD NAMES
Billy-biter; pick-cheese; blue top; tittymouse

Feisty things often come in tiny packages. The blue tit measures just 12cm, but possesses a temperament the inverse of its size. During nesting they're intolerant of anything 'not quite right', think and fly in straight lines, and get a proper grump on if other blue tits muscle in on their area. The trees in our garden offer a home to a pair and, despite having long seen off any real rivals, they still spend countless hours exploding in rage. The problem is that the birds they're so furious about are themselves: the ones they imagine to be on the other side of car wing-mirrors, which they merrily attempt to bully away. If the line between genius and madness is thin, blue tits are perched right on the fence.

Remarkably for such tiny birds, they lay between seven and 16 eggs and feed their young mainly with moth caterpillars – an average brood requires as many as 1,000 caterpillars a day. The British population is estimated at 3 million pairs, producing around 30 million young per year. It's a wonder there are any moths left at all.

Once the scourge of milk-loving families across Britain, blue tits learned to peck through the foil caps of doorstep-left milk, enticed by the fat-rich cream that settled towards the top of the bottle. The fast spread of this phenomenon across Britain led some to claim it as a kind of magic. But the truth is simpler: observed behaviour, passed on from parent to offspring, led to a rapid evolution of diet and conduct. Now, as we move towards skimmed and semi-skimmed milk, and away from morning milk deliveries, it's a ritual likely to soon pass into myth.

Blackbird

Turdus merula

FAMILY
Turdidae – thrushes

HABITAT
Towns, gardens, parks – wherever there are trees or bushes

SIZE
24–25cm long

DIET
Worms, insects, berries

BREEDS
March–August, two to four broods

NEST
Cup of grass and leaves

EGGS
Four to five. Light blue

RANGE
Everywhere in the UK

COLLECTIVE NOUN
Cloud

OLD NAMES
Amsel; oossel; colley; black thrush; blackie

The blackbird is a member of the thrush family. The males are black with a yellow beak, the females brownish with a dark beak. They are ground feeders particularly fond of worms, and a common visitor to gardens. And, despite having two eyes, they like to use just one at a time.

You may be familiar with the scene: a blackbird appears on a fence post. Another blackbird appears on a fence post on the opposite side of the garden. Each is agitated by the other's presence and makes a few hops and turns on the spot, accompanied by clicking calls. Eventually one grows bored/brave enough to drop down to the grass, cocking its head to peer at the ground with one eye, at which point the other blackbird swoops in and chases its rival out of the area. After briefly savouring its victory, the triumphant blackbird realises that another bird has encroached on the fence post it abandoned and hostilities recommence.

Blackbirds are very territorial and generally solitary. They rarely tolerate other blackbirds, except when food is scarce. They're always on the lookout for other blackbirds and more dangerous visitors, such as cats and sparrowhawks. In fact they're so watchful, they can sleep with one eye open. Blackbirds are among those animals known to exhibit unihemispheric slow-wave sleep, allowing them to switch off one half of their brain but keep the other half on standby. Blackbirds signal their territory by singing, using a variety of tonally distinctive vocalisations. They have even been known to do this while roosting at night, continually reminding other blackbirds who your garden belongs to.

So, humble as they initially appear, the next time you see a blackbird, remember that it is feisty, a bit squinty and can sing in its sleep.

Wren

Troglodytes troglodytes

FAMILY
Troglodytidae – wrens

HABITAT
Gardens, hedges and woods

SIZE
9–10cm long

DIET
Insects

BREEDS
April–May, one to two broods

NEST
Dome of moss, grass and leaves

EGGS
Five to eight. White with red speckles

RANGE
Most abundant bird in the UK. Found all across Europe

COLLECTIVE NOUN
Chime

OLD NAMES
Jenny wren; creeper; chitty; our lady's hen; stinkie

One of the smallest of British birds (though not the tiniest of the lot – that honour goes to the firecrests and goldcrests) and possibly the most abundant. It is estimated there could be as many as 17 million wrens in the UK, though you're less likely to see one than a robin, blackbird or house sparrow. Wherever you are, you're probably never far from a wren – you can recognise it by its unexpectedly loud song as it chatters away, hidden in a bush, upright tail frantically bobbing about.

Eurasian wrens reside in their own taxonomic family – the *Troglodytidaes*. The name comes from a Greek word for 'cave dweller' as wrens have a tendency to hide away in nooks and crannies. It's something Wordsworth alluded to in his poem 'A Wren's Nest': "*And when for their abodes they seek/An opportune recess,/The hermit has no finer eye/For shadowy quietness*". Think of a wren like an airborne mouse and you won't be far off either in size or twitchy behaviour.

Male wrens take on the responsibility of nest building, constructing several in various places, before showing the female around to take her pick. Once selected, the female then sets about the interior decoration, lining it with feathers and hair. The unused nests – also known as 'cock-nests' – are not wholly abandoned as they are used later by the couple and their young as occasional sleeping shelters.

In the past wrens have also been known as 'kinglets' – now the family name for firecrests and goldcrests – probably stemming from an old fable about a wren that hid in the feathers of an eagle, hitching a lift to win the 'whoever-flies-highest-becomes-king of the birds' competition, popping out at the last minute to claim the prize.

Robin

Erithacus rubecula

FAMILY
Muscicapidae – Old World
flycatchers

HABITAT
Gardens, hedges and woods

SIZE
13–15cm long

DIET
Insects

BREEDS
April–June, two to three broods

NEST
Cup low down on ground,
hedge or tree

EGGS
Five to six. White with red speckles

RANGE
Found all across Europe
apart from Iceland

COLLECTIVE NOUN
Round

OLD NAMES
Redbreast; ploughman's bird;
ruddock; bobby

Allegedly, the robin is Britain's national bird. Which is a shame. Not that there's anything wrong with robins, it's just that they're a bit of an obvious choice. It was elected to the post in a public vote organised by David Lindo, the Urban Birder, but if the poll had been restricted to the UK's six million or so active birdwatchers, the result may have been different. For what it's worth, my vote went to the hen harrier. Anyway…

When I was growing up I was taught that robins were members of the thrush family, but at some point they left that and joined the flycatchers, which makes sense given that they look more like the latter than the former. In fact kicking the interlopers out of the family wasn't just some random act of pique, but down to DNA analysis.

The place you're most likely to see robins? Christmas cards. But they're also year-round visitors to our gardens. The hardy British robin is an almost unique offshoot among its European cousins in that it doesn't migrate to Africa for winter. It has come to be associated with Christmas because of its ubiquity during winter and its ability to keep belting out the tunes in even the harshest of weather.

Robins are small birds with a most ferocious temper, a pointy beak and a bright orange breast. Back in the day we didn't have a name for orange – the word only turned up in English after actual oranges did – so the birds were simply known as 'redbreasts'.

Song thrush

Turdus philomelos

FAMILY
Turdidae – thrushes

HABITAT
Woodland, gardens and hedges

SIZE
23cm long

DIET
Snails, berries and earthworms

BREEDS
March–July, two to three broods

NEST
Grassy cup

EGGS
Three to five. Light blue

RANGE
Found across Europe,
apart from Iceland

COLLECTIVE NOUN
Hermitage

OLD NAMES
Throstle; thrusher; throggy;
mavie; garden thrush

Thrushes come in all shapes and sizes, and some aren't even called thrushes at all. The blackbird is a thrush, as are redwings, fieldfares, ring ouzels and – until recently – so, too, were robins. The 'actual' thrushes you see in your garden are likely one of two varieties: song or mistle thrushes. The two are closely related and at first glance appear similar, but can be told apart by season, size, sound, setting and behaviour.

Thrushes are known for being dotty across their chests. Mistle thrushes are not only bigger than their singing cousins, but also have a different type of spot – a splodgy dot rather than the song thrush's upwards-facing arrow-head. Get close enough to have a good look and it should be visible.

But their behaviours are totally different, too. You're most likely to spot a song thrush in spring, perched at the top of a tree and singing its elaborate and beautiful song. Not only is its song complicated, but it's also loud: song thrushes have among the biggest volume-to-size ratios of any bird. Meanwhile, mistle thrushes are most often seen in winter, descending on berried trees to claim them as their own. They'll angrily chase away any birds that dare come near and generally let out an irritating machine-gun 'clack, clack, clack' rattle.

Colloquially, song thrushes are known as the 'gardener's friend'. They have a particular appetite for snails and are one of the few birds to use tools. After picking up a snail, they'll take it to their favourite 'anvil' – usually a suitably positioned and shaped rock – and beat the living hell out of it. If you discover a rock in your garden surrounded by broken snail shells, you're fortunate to have a thrush prone to song nearby.

Tree sparrow

Passer montanus

FAMILY
Passeridae – Old World sparrows

HABITAT
Woodland edges

SIZE
14cm long

DIET
Seeds

BREEDS
April–July, two to three broods

NEST
Hole in tree or nest box

EGGS
Four to six. White/pale grey
with brown blotches

RANGE
Found sparsely across the UK

COLLECTIVE NOUN
Stand

OLD NAMES
Chocolate head; rock sparrow;
mountain sparrow; copper nob

We all know sparrows. They're the classic and ubiquitous 'little brown jobs' that seem to be everywhere – probably among the first birds we learn to identify, and among the first we learn to ignore. Chances are the sparrows you spot in your garden are house sparrows, but there's also another kind – rarer, endangered, more delicate, and so worthy of interest they get even the most world-weary of birdwatchers twitching.

There are three main ways to tell tree and house sparrows apart. First, the latter aren't large, but tree sparrows are significantly smaller. Second, house sparrows are strongly sexually dimorphic – males and females look different – while tree sparrows are monomorphic. So, while male house sparrows have a dark brown cap and females are an inconspicuous mix of mottled browns, all tree sparrows sport chestnut caps, looking much like tiny male house sparrows. However, the clearest way to differentiate the two species is to look at their cheeks, where tree sparrows have a distinctive squarish-shaped dot.

While their cousins may be inescapable, the UK's tree sparrow population has plummeted by over 90 per cent since the 1970s. But you can do your bit. Tree sparrows are social nesters that like to live in small colonies of five or six families. If you spot them in your garden, try putting up a few nest boxes. We put a handful up a while ago and every year since get to watch wave after wave of baby tree sparrows fledging throughout spring and summer. When my uncle, a committed birdwatcher, comes to visit he has been known to jump out of the running car with binoculars already raised to get a look. So, always take notice of those little brown jobs. One or two might be so exotic and precious as to make a dedicated birder's heart race a little faster.

Starling

Sturnus vulgaris

FAMILY
Sturnidae – starlings

HABITAT
Everywhere

SIZE
20–22cm long

DIET
Mostly insects

BREEDS
April–July, one to two broods

NEST
Hole in a tree or building

EGGS
Five to seven. Pale blue

RANGE
Resident, boosted by additional birds in winter from Scandinavia

COLLECTIVE NOUN
Chattering or murmuration

OLD NAMES
Black felt; dusky thrush; jester bird; horse sparrow; sheppie

Starlings are famous for their murmurations in which swirling masses swarm above their nesting trees in autumn and winter. Flocks can number in their hundreds of thousands, and be very noisy and whiffy. How they don't all collide into each other is a miracle. But there's safety in numbers: congregating in large groups helps scare off any peregrine falcon in the area. Just as importantly, it allows starlings to create a huge information network about the best feeding grounds – as well as giving us something to gawp at in wonder during the wintry twilight.

Starlings generally feed upon subterranean invertebrates and – when not squawking from a tree or lamppost – can be seen scurrying around the ground. They use a probing technique, plunging their long pointed beaks deep into the earth and then opening their jaws to create a hole.

From a distance they may look like small, dark nondescript birds, but closer inspection reveals beautiful iridescent flecks of green and purple, and white spots amid their plumage. The colours help starlings pick a mate, as the stronger the colours, the healthier the bird.

Starlings are in the same family as mynah birds and share their ability for mimicry. This can be heard in their songs, which as well as the noises of other birds, can include more urban sounds such as power drills, telephones and sirens. The birds that occasionally nest in our garden have learnt to mimic a buzzard, probably to scare off other birds and claim the patch as their own. Mozart once taught a starling to sing his 'Piano Concerto No.17 in G Major'. Despite the fact the bird erroneously sang in G sharp, Mozart kept it as a pet until its death, upon which he gave it a full burial ceremony and wrote a commemorative poem.

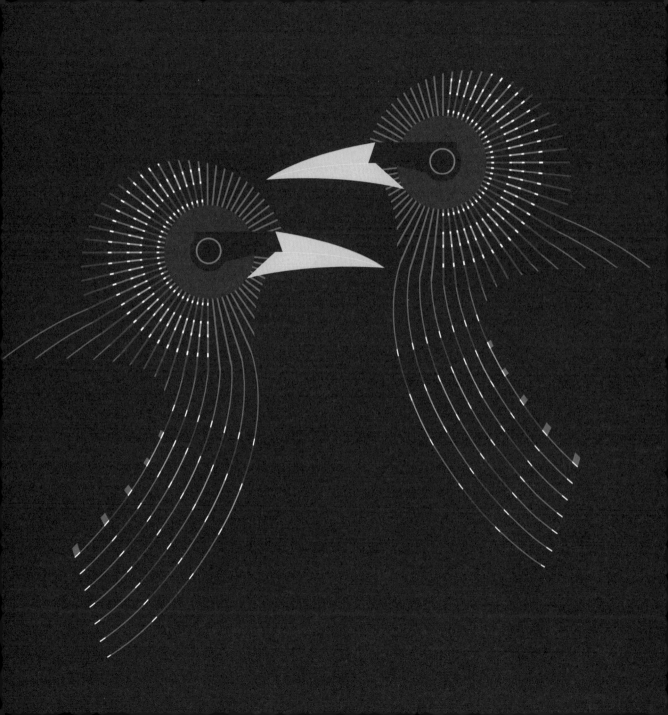

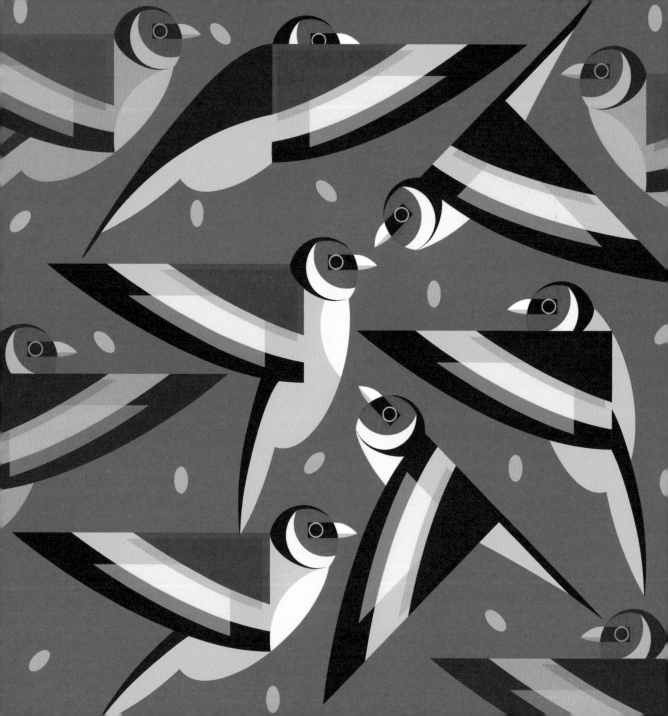

Goldfinch

Carduelis carduelis

FAMILY
Fringillidae – true finches

HABITAT
Gardens, orchards and
cultivated farmland

SIZE
12–13cm long

DIET
Small seeds, thistle, teasel, nyjer

BREEDS
May–July, two broods

NEST
Neat nest of roots and cobwebs

EGGS
Five to six. Very pale blue
with reddish speckles

RANGE
Present throughout Britain
and Europe, except Iceland
and northern Scandinavia

COLLECTIVE NOUN
Charm

OLD NAMES
Jack-a-nickas; gowdspink; nicker
nocker; thistlewarp; speckled dick;
seven-coloured linnet

Given how much we venerate gold, it's odd how this bird's name does it such little justice. The collective noun of 'charm' fits, but the 'gold' tag is barely descriptive – apart from two yellow stripes on its wings, it expresses neither its sparkling appearance, its flight nor its song. In reality the goldfinch is an airborne Mondrian, whirling angular splashes of black, white, yellow and red, accompanied by a telltale tinkling chatter. The old-fangled names of red-fronted thistle finch, seven-coloured linnet and lady with the twelve flounces provide more colour, but that colour definitely isn't gold.

Goldfinches are unmistakeable birds, but perhaps prompt more 'what's that?' comments than most. That's likely because they've recently become more frequent after a century of decline. Catching and caging wild birds was once a common pastime and goldfinches experienced the bulk of the suffering – hundreds of thousands of them were caught each year for the pet trade. The RSPB and various acts of parliament finally brought the practice to an end but, having escaped persecution from capture, farming methods changed around them, decimating crucial environments and food supplies, and their numbers continued to plummet.

So, for generations they became unfamiliar. But now they're spiralling back, and it's largely down to us. Over the past two decades, more people have taken to filling feeders and graduated from generic feed to bird-specific seed. In the case of goldfinches, we've replaced their lost habitats of thistle and teasel with feeders full of nyjer, and are helping them thrive. Alongside that resurgence comes reacquaintance as our gardens once again fill with their very Edwardian charm of colour and noise. Even so, they're still not gold…

Chaffinch

Fringilla coelebs

FAMILY
Fringillidae – finches

HABITAT
Woodland, gardens, parks

SIZE
14cm long

DIET
Insects, caterpillars, seeds and berries

BREEDS
April–May, one brood

NEST
Cup of grass and leaves

EGGS
Four to five. Blue to red-grey

RANGE
Widespread across Europe

COLLECTIVE NOUN
Charm

OLD NAMES
French linnet; charbob; pea finch; pink-pink; taggyfinch

Occasionally, it's nice to go on holiday with friends rather than family. This happens in the bird world, too, and there's even a fancy name for it: differential migration. Most chaffinches do it every winter: the males migrate just a short distance from their breeding grounds, while the females travel further south. In the absence of mates, the males are left to cluster together in large flocks, hence the species' Latin name, *Fringilla coelebs*, which means 'bachelor bird'. Their common name comes from their habit of eating the chaff that used to fall out of horses' nose bags.

Chaffinches are our most commonly seen finch and can be found in gardens at any time of year. But their migratory habits mean it's probably not the same birds you're seeing from season to season. The large flocks that gather on British farmland are often Scandinavian immigrants, their numbers swelling when the beech mast crop has proved insufficient across Europe. The native population is boosted by around 10 million continental birds over winter, which travel alongside smaller numbers of the closely related brambling.

Male chaffinches are colourful, with a grey mantle and pink and red underparts, while the females are more brownish. Both genders have long, forked tales and a distinctive white crossbar on their wings.

Originally a woodland bird, chaffinches have now branched out into many habitats. They're a common visitor to gardens and are one of the most numerous birds in Britain. Because of this it is important to keep your birdfeeders clean as chaffinches have been known to carry the deadly trichomonosis parasite, causing falls not just in chaffinch numbers but those of other species, too, particularly the greenfinch.

Bullfinch

Pyrrhula pyrrhula

FAMILY
Fringillidae – finches

HABITAT
Woodland, gardens, parks

SIZE
15cm long

DIET
Buds, berries and leaves

BREEDS
July–September, two broods

NEST
Cup in a bush or low tree

EGGS
Four to five. Greenish-blue

RANGE
Found across temperate Europe,
but less so in hot and cold places

COLLECTIVE NOUN
Bellowing

OLD NAMES
Black-headed bully; blood-olph;
monk; plum-budder; bull spink

You're unlikely to see a bullfinch in your garden at any time other than winter. They're a secretive woodland bird for most of the year, only brave enough to go looking for food near us when it gets properly chilly. Which makes this next point slightly redundant: bullfinches can appear to be brighter and bigger in winter. It's neither an optical illusion, nor a change in their appearance. The truth is that we receive visiting birds from the continent in the colder months and they are bolder in size, colour and behaviour than our resident British birds.

Nevertheless, whether they're visiting or native, bullfinches are very dapper birds with black caps, grey mantles, black wings and distinctive white rumps. Males sport a red breast, while the female's is greyish pink, and both are front loaded and top heavy, with ample chests, flat, almost neckless heads, and stubby small beaks.

Bullfinches stay in pairs in which the female is dominant. They don't gallivant around in large raucous flocks like other finches, and you'll generally spot a solitary couple. Compared to other finches, and given their bold colouring and impressive size, it's surprising that bullfinches are such secretive birds – even their voice is a timid 'peeuuw'.

During summer, bullfinches develop food pouches in their mouth, allowing them to store insects to feed their young. But their bills are designed for devouring the tree and fruit buds they enjoy most. In fact they love fruit buds so much that there was once a bounty on bullfinches in Britain as they were considered an agricultural pest. From the 1950s onwards, thousands were trapped on fruit farms. Since the 1970s, numbers have dwindled, probably as a result of intensive farming and habitat loss, and have now only just begun to recover.

Greenfinch

Chloris chloris

FAMILY
Fringillidae – finches

HABITAT
Gardens, hedges and woods

SIZE
13–15cm long

DIET
Seeds and berries

BREEDS
April–June, two to three broods

NEST
Cup in hedge

EGGS
Four to six. White to pale
blue with red speckles

RANGE
Widespread across the UK,
migrants joining in winter

COLLECTIVE NOUN
Trembling

OLD NAMES
Barley bird; green chub;
green lintie; green olph

The greenfinch has grey and yellow plumage, but from a distance takes on a very green tint. It's a large seed-eating finch, once a common garden visitor and often seen singing on rooftops or sat atop hedgerows. When they visit feeders, you'll notice they like to bully their way on to perches and sit there eating for a considerable time, much to the dismay of smaller birds. Like those of other finches, their numbers swell in winter and flocks of hundreds can be spotted on telegraph lines. Despite this, greenfinches are not as numerous as they once were…

In 2005 UK chaffinches and greenfinches were blighted by an epidemic of trichomonosis that saw chaffinch numbers drop by seven per cent and greenfinch numbers depleted by an enormous 35 per cent in two years. Trichomonosis is a disease caused by the Trichomonas gallinae parasite, and had long been associated with doves, pigeons and raptors but spread widely to finches. It has now also started to affect house sparrows, yellowhammers, great tits and other songbirds. Diseased birds can appear fat, lethargic, unwilling to fly and have moisture around their beaks.

Disease can be easily communicated at feeding stations, which makes it important to keep bird-feeding areas clean. Feeders and bird baths should be scrubbed thoroughly using a five per cent disinfectant solution, soaked and then air dried regularly. Only fill feeders with enough food to last a couple of days. Do not place food directly on the ground – instead use ground feeders – clear waste and droppings, and keep grass cut short. Move your feeders around the garden so that you do not get a build-up of droppings. It may sound like a lot of work but your greenfinches will be grateful.

Great tit

Parus major

FAMILY
Paridae – tits

HABITAT
Woodland, gardens and parks

SIZE
14cm long

DIET
Insects, seeds, nuts and berries

BREEDS
April–May, one to two broods

NEST
Hole in tree or nest box

EGGS
Five to 11. White, speckled red

RANGE
All of Europe, apart from Iceland

COLLECTIVE NOUN
Dissimulation

OLD NAMES
Bee biter; black-headed tomtit;
pick cheese; tinker; tom tit

Of all the tits likely to visit your garden, the great tit, as the name suggests, is the largest. Boxy and muscular, it's noticeably larger, darker and more yellowy-green than a blue tit. That yellow colouring, which runs either side of a central dark stripe down its chest, is produced by a carotenoid-rich diet and is a sign of health to potential mates. The same mechanism turns flamingos pink, but in great tits the closer it gets to a rich lemony-yellow, the better its diet and the better mate it will find.

The great tit's greatest trick is its versatile – and very loud – voice. Most birds have a select repertoire of songs, clicks and whistles that they repeat endlessly to attract a mate or mark out a territory. Great tits, on the other hand, have a potential vocal arsenal of around 70 different calls and songs, although individual birds tend to limit those to under ten personal greatest hits. The reason is the so-called 'Beau Geste hypothesis': by hopping from place to place and singing a repeated variety of tunes from different locations, great tits try to make out their territory is full to the gunnels with angry tits ready to defend it to the hilt, and thus no place for others to take up residence.

The elephant in the room is the species' innuendo-tastic name. Great tits are perhaps the most amusingly named of all birds – at least in Britain. Elsewhere in the bird world you have the joys of seeking out the equally ludicrous-sounding penduline tits, frilled coquettes, blue-footed boobies and bearded helmetcrests. Tread carefully, however: start joking about great tits in front of a serious birdwatcher and chances are you'll receive a look telling you it's not big and it's not clever.

Coal tit

Periparus ater

FAMILY
Paridae – tits, chickadees and titmice

HABITAT
Woods, hedges and gardens

SIZE
10–12cm long

DIET
Insects and seeds

BREEDS
April–May, one to two broods

NEST
Hole in a tree

EGGS
Seven to nine. White with red speckles

RANGE
Common across Britain and Europe, but less recognised than other tits

COLLECTIVE NOUN
Banditry

OLD NAMES
Coal titmouse; black ox-eye; coaly hood; cole mouse; little blackcap; underground tit

In 1758 the Swedish botanist Carl Linnaeus tried to jazz up the name of this tiny tit by calling it *Parus capite nigro: vertice albo dorso cinereo pectore albo*, a tongue twister that means 'black-headed tit with white nape, ash-grey back and white breast'. Fortunately, the bird already had a shorter, snappier name so it didn't catch on. However, top marks to Linnaeus for highlighting the distinctive white stripe on the back of its head – and for saving me from having to nail an accurate description.

While noted as a bird of coniferous woodland, this minor tit is one of the most frequently seen in British gardens. Coal tits are busy and noisy, hurtling to a feeder for a quick beak-grab of food, then retreating to a safe perch to eat at leisure or cache away for later. Their song is faster and higher pitched than that of the great tit and can sound like the 'dee-dah dee-dah' of a siren. They can often be heard or seen in small groups, particularly in winter when they gather with their larger tit cousins.

Genetically, they are most closely related to the chickadees and titmice of North America and their range spans from Britain through Europe, to northern Africa, the Himalayas and other parts of Asia. Coal tits do not migrate – however, if the weather gets really bad, they might pack their bags and clear off somewhere warmer for a few weeks. They like to nest in tree cavities, rotting stumps and disused animal burrows, which might explain why their nests (like those of other tits) are so often infested with fleas. While unhygienic, this does have the advantage of stopping unwanted visits from neighbours and family. Not a tactic we recommend trying at home, however.

Long-tailed tit

Aegithalos caudatus

FAMILY
Aegithalidae – bushtits

HABITAT
Hedgerows, gardens, bushy areas
and mixed woodland

SIZE
13–15cm long, including tail

DIET
Insects and seeds

BREEDS
April–May, one brood

NEST
An oval ball-like structure with an
entrance hole. Built by both sexes.
Weaving hair, moss, feathers
and cobwebs from the inside.
Decorated with lichen

EGGS
Eight to 12. White with reddish
marks

RANGE
Most of Europe except far north

COLLECTIVE NOUN
Volery

OLD NAMES
Bum barrel; bell ringer;
feather bed; nimble tailor

Tintinnabulation. Not a word you'll use every day – it means the sound of tiny tinkling bells – but it provides a first inkling of what a gang of small pink-tinted fluff balls gathering in your garden sounds like. Oddly, for such a cute bird, the long-tailed tit's old and local names are rather less enchanting: bum barrel, mumruffin, bum towel, oven bird. But in the end that somehow only makes them sound more adorable.

For most birds, the songs we think of as 'pretty' are in fact the avian equivalent of shouting "Oi! Get off my land!" or "I'm feeling fruity". But the endless falsetto chatter of long-tailed tits tends to be just family members checking in with each other. They travel around in familial groups – mainly nuclear families of 12 or so – but sometimes uncles, aunts and cousins are invited into gatherings of up to 50. Close family is probably important to them as they're not really tits at all – they're Europe's lonely babblers, all the rest of which are in Asia.

Being near to siblings must also be a confidence booster as they're surprisingly happy to get close to humans. If they do alight in your garden, it'll be by swarm – stand under an invaded tree and they'll be flitting and tinkling just over your head. And if you're lucky enough to spy them sleeping, you'll witness a super-bundle of pink fluffiness as the family huddles together to keep warm. Their nests – even fluffier than the birds themselves – can be attended by more than one couple, with uncles, aunts and siblings busying themselves with bringing up their relatives' young. If you're a long-tailed tit, it's *all* about family.

Wood pigeon

Columba palumbus

FAMILY
Columbidae – pigeons and doves

HABITAT
Woodland, gardens and parks

SIZE
40cm long

DIET
Leaves, berries and fruit

BREEDS
All year, up to six broods

NEST
Platform in tree

EGGS
Two. White

RANGE
Found across western Europe

COLLECTIVE NOUN
Band

OLD NAMES
Clatter dove; cowscot; oodal; cushie doo

Wherever you are, you're probably near a pigeon. In towns and cities they're regarded as pests, but these urban pigeons are almost exclusively feral ancestors of the rock dove – escapees from dovecotes that have adapted from their natural habitat of rocky cliffs to the artificial cliff faces offered by high-rises, office blocks and churches. But in parks and the countryside, there's a different pigeon: barrel-chested, more colourful, just a fraction more charming, though also regarded as a pest, and likely the largest bird to regularly visit your garden.

Wood pigeons are large, slatey blue-grey birds with patches of white on their necks, a variety of streaks and iridescent purple and green running through their plumage, and prone to some serious cooing. And some serious cooking. Pigeon pie was once a popular dish in the UK – at least until the late 19th century when a bad pie poisoned a troop ship, 'squab' flew off the menu, and dovecotes fell out of favour as food stores.

Wood pigeons are unusual among British birds in that they breed at any time of year. The height of summer is preferable, but they'll produce up to six clutches in a 12-month period. This is in part due to the low survival rates of young pigeons, with most not making it throughs their first year. Whether it's falling from a tree, or being such large, clumsy and poor flyers that they become meals for sparrowhawks and goshawks, it's a perilous existence for a young woody.

Almost entirely vegetarian, wood pigeons survive on a diet of acorns, seeds, leaves and grains. An adaptation, shared with some flamingos and penguins, allows them to convert food stored in their crop, a pouch in their digestive system, into a nutrient-rich gloop known as 'crop milk'. The parents then feed their hatchlings on this until they fledge.

Birds of the Countryside

Not all birds are so obliging as to visit your garden. In the woods, across the fields and country lanes, even in suburban parks, there are many more specialist, sometimes timid, often stubborn birds to spot. Some have travelled great distances from both north and south; others literally live their lives upside down. You just need to go for a walk to find them.

Barn swallow

Hirundo rustica

FAMILY
Hirundinidae – swallows and martins

HABITAT
Open countryside with farms, ponds, meadows, usually near buildings for nesting

SIZE
17–19cm long

DIET
Insects

BREEDS
April–August, two broods

NEST
Mud and straw cup

EGGS
Four to six. White with reddish speckles

RANGE
Summer visitor across the whole of the UK. Winters in South Africa

COLLECTIVE NOUN
Kettle

OLD NAMES
Chimney swallow; swallie; tsi-kuk

Fluttering and flapping, swooping and soaring, the barn swallow is the herald of summer, a champion long-distance flier and sometime sky gypsy. It uses its proficient aerial abilities to undertake an astonishing annual roundtrip of 12,500 miles, all for the sake of healthily bringing up its offspring.

Wintering in South Africa before returning to Britain to breed in April, swallows build their homes in their same favourite barns or other outbuildings year after year. As with other migratory birds, we tend to imagine them as visitors, but they're really birds with two homes, revisiting each during their respective summertimes to make the most of available food sources. Depending on whether they're hurtling high or low, they take insects on the wing in their pouch-like mouths or swoop over ponds to scoop up water to drink. If you're a swallow, you do everything on the wing.

Towards the end of summer, you often see swallows gathering on high lines, chattering excitedly to one another. These are normally family groups, with the parents likely passing on 'fill your bellies' instructions to their young before their first long trip to Africa. Swallows are similar to swifts in appearance, migration and behaviour and the two can sometimes be mistaken – the telltale sign of a swallow is its forked tail (the word 'swallow' literally means 'cleft stick'). But the two originated from entirely separate families, with the wondrous logic of evolution converging on similar conclusions from dissimilar starting points.

Yellowhammer

Emberiza citrinella

FAMILY
Emberizidae – buntings

HABITAT
Heaths and farmland

SIZE
16cm long

DIET
Insects and seeds

BREEDS
April–July, two to three broods

NEST
Cup on the ground under a hedge

EGGS
Three to five. Pale with
scribbled markings

RANGE
Found across Europe, apart from
areas of extreme heat or cold

COLLECTIVE NOUN
Decoration

OLD NAMES
Bessy; devil's bird; gladdie; scribble
master; scribble car; scribbling
schoolmaster; scribble lark

Yellowhammers are by far the yellowest of British birds. If you've never seen one, you might be shocked when you do: against a ruddy black-streaked body, their yellow heads and chests are so yellow they're almost fluorescent. The closest thing to the yellow of a yellowhammer is a high-vis jacket, but high-vis not being a thing in the 19th century, John Clare plumped for *"yellow breast and head of solid gold"* in his poem about the bird.

As buntings, yellowhammers are loosely related to finches and can generally be seen through spring and summer on the peripheries of fields and nearby gardens, but rarely, if ever, in towns. The tops of hedges are their favourite haunts but – surprisingly, given how bright they are – you'll almost certainly hear one before you see it. We often think of swallows as the symbols of oncoming summer but, to me at least, the yellowhammer's song is the first sign that things are warming up. Enid Blyton popularised the idea that their call sounds like they're asking for a *"little bit of bread and no cheese"*, but where I live in the north of Scotland they normally run out of steam before they get to the cheese. Even if you've never heard it, the yellowhammer's song might sound familiar as, according to one of the composer's pupils, it inspired the opening notes of Beethoven's Fifth Symphony.

One traditional name for the yellowhammer was the scribble lark, on account of the inky lines scrawled across its eggs that help provide camouflage in its low hedgerow nest. Those lines were once believed to be the work of the devil – a cryptically satanic message so diabolical that the birds themselves were persecuted.

Blackcap

Sylvia atricapilla

FAMILY
Sylviidae – typical warblers

HABITAT
Open woodland, increasingly gardens

SIZE
13cm long

DIET
Berries and insects

BREEDS
April–July, one to two broods

NEST
Cup in bushes

EGGS
Four to five. Off white with darker spots

RANGE
Once a summer visitor, increasingly resident all year around

COLLECTIVE NOUN
Confusion

OLD NAMES
Guernsey nightingale; nettle creeper; blackbonnet; peggy

The blackcap is a small grey songbird from the warbler family with a coloured cap on its head. Only males sport the black one, though. Unusually for birds, female blackcaps are the dandier of the two sexes, wearing rusty red bonnets. In general – although not exclusively – female birds do the egg sitting and tend to evolve a drabber appearance that provides better camouflage. Meanwhile, males have to compete for mates and usually have brighter, more extravagant and foppish colours and behaviours. This can lead to extreme differences, such as the distinct colouring of the male and female hen harriers. But there are exceptions, such as the phalarope, which switches the usual parenting roles.

Many guide books will tell you that blackcaps, like other warblers, are summer and passage visitors to the UK and absent through the colder months. But if that is the case, why are blackcaps popping into our gardens in increasing numbers over winter?

The answer is that our summer visitors – which winter in North Africa and the Middle East – leave the country in the autumn and are then replaced by blackcaps that have migrated from further north for our winter. However, recently a number of birds from central Europe have stopped flying south and begun heading west towards British gardens.

Climate change making our winters less harsh is part of the cause. But it's also linked to our rising use of birdfeeders. Historically, warblers would rarely visit bird tables, but if mealworms are on the menu in your garden, you could be rewarded by a visit from one of these elusive birds, which could have arrived from the north, south, east, or simply be a resident.

Redwing

Turdus iliacus

FAMILY
Turdidae – thrushes

HABITAT
Woodland, heaths, fields
and occasionally gardens

SIZE
20–22cm long

DIET
Berries and insects

BREEDS
April–June, two broods

NEST
Cup built against tree, they
tend to be quite low down

EGGS
Four to five. Pale blue with
brown speckles

RANGE
Winter visitor to UK. Summers
in Scandinavia and Iceland

COLLECTIVE NOUN
Mutation

OLD NAMES
Feller; Norway nightingale;
storm bird; wind thrush

You might not know it, but every autumn the UK is invaded by a Viking horde. Lining up at dusk on the coastlines of Scandinavia and Iceland, millions of ravenous marauders set off on a properly perilous 500-mile journey across the sea. When they arrive they hide away in woods and forests, sending out raiding parties of 20 to 30 to pillage what they can, noisily 'see-ip'-ing their high-pitched call in unison. Their plunder? The berries of country gardens.

The redwing is the smallest of UK thrushes, easily mistaken for a song thrush and slightly smaller than a blackbird. But what it lacks in stature, it makes up for by working as a team – most thrushes, in contrast, tend to be solitary. If you're fortunate enough to see them, they really are unmistakable, partly by the size of their flocks. However, they are slightly misnamed: their wings aren't really that red – they're more of a red armpit. Gangs of redwings can completely overwhelm a suitable tree. They love berries and, observing them in our garden, we've noticed they seem to prefer rowan, have a taste for holly and – when they've stripped those bare – will settle for yew. And then they're off to maraud somebody else's bush.

As thrushes, they belong to the family *Turdidae* and often travel with their much larger Scandi cousin, the fieldfare. The surprising thing about both species is that despite invading in their millions, they're so wary of humans that you're unlikely to see them unless you live out in the country or, at a push, the edge of a village. If there's a truly Baltic spell, they might venture into towns, but it's rare. Rarer still are the redwings that stay in Britain over the summer. Of the million or so that make the annual trip from the north, fewer than 20 pairs don't bother to go back.

Tawny owl

Strix aluco

FAMILY
Strigidae – true owls

HABITAT
Woodland

SIZE
36–40cm long

DIET
Voles, mice and frogs

BREEDS
April–June, one brood

NEST
Hole in tree

EGGS
Two to five. White

RANGE
Resident throughout Europe, apart from northern Scandinavia

COLLECTIVE NOUN
Parliament

OLD NAMES
Billy hooter; gilly houter; wood owl; yewlatt; beech owl

The tawny owl is the most common owl in Britain, but it's more familiar to us by sound than sight. Its call is what most of us would think of as the 'classic owl noise', a slightly mispronounced 'twit-twooing'. You've probably heard the 'hoo-hooing' hoot of the male at night or the female's screeching 'ki-wek' response. Tawny owls like their own space, but don't like moving about, so they generally rely on their hoots to maintain their territories. On chilly autumn nights, the countryside can be filled with the sound of hooing and ki-weking from all directions as tawnies lay claim to their patches.

Tawny owls mate for life, but out of the mating season, pairs tend to keep their distance. If you find an owl nest, it's best not to approach as tawnies are fiercely protective and will attack intruders, usually going for the head. Once owlets are old enough not to fall out of trees, they are chased off their parents' territory to fend for themselves.

Tawny owls are highly nocturnal yet their eyes are no more sensitive to light than our own. But then they don't need sight to move around in the dark – their world is governed by sound. Tawnies' ears are highly sensitive and placed asymmetrically on their heads, allowing them to judge the distance and direction of sounds and hone in on their prey – mainly small rodents. Tawny owls' ears are covered by feathers that are constructed so as not to block sound. They also don't like rain as it plays havoc with their sensitive ears – a damp owl is not a happy one.

Tawny owls are stout birds with streaky brown plumage, large black eyes and rounded wings. They're not the best flyers: they prefer to perch at a listening post and pounce on their unsuspecting prey, emitting the odd screech or hoot to keep the neighbours away.

Kestrel

Falco tinnunculus

FAMILY
Falconidae – falcons and caracaras

HABITAT
Woodland, heaths and roadsides

SIZE
35–40cm long

DIET
Voles, mice, small birds

BREEDS
March–July, one brood

NEST
Various: from buildings
to disused crow nests

EGGS
Four to six. White with
red/brown speckles

RANGE
Found across Europe

COLLECTIVE NOUN
Flight

OLD NAMES
Blood hawk; keelie; willy whip;
windhover; mouse hawk

Think of an immovable object and many things might come to mind – a rock, an elephant or a building. But probably not a small, elegant falcon. If the wind could speak, however, it would be swift to explain that kestrels are the epitome of things it cannot budge. Although designed to move forward in flight, by rapidly flapping their tapered wings and balancing with their long tails, these petite raptors can pin themselves in the air, defying whatever the elements throw at them.

Kestrels are widespread in Britain – often spotted by roads, hovering just 20 metres above the ground. This allows them to hold their heads still and look for shiny ultra-violet traces of vole urine. Other mammals, birds, reptiles and worms are on the menu, but voles are a kestrel's absolute favourite and they like to eat about half a dozen a day. Kestrels do not chase their prey and when not hovering and dropping on to their victims, they're perched on branches or telephone poles waiting to pounce.

Growing up on the edge of suburbia in the early 1970s, almost any glance up to the sky would reveal a windhover – as kestrels are also known – rebuffing the wind over nearby fields. But, for me at least, such sights became part of a half-remembered childhood. Being so tied to voles means kestrel populations fluctuate from year to year, but over the past four decades, numbers have crashed and the species has moved from a familiar sight to a place on the amber list of conservation concern. In Scotland numbers have fallen by over 65 per cent in 20 years.

Kestrels lay their eggs in disused bird nests or on human-made sites. These pretty raptors have predominantly orange plumage, covered in black-and-white specks and spots, with males differentiated by their grey caps. Kestrels get their name from their shrill cry of 'kee! kee! kee!'

Great spotted woodpecker

Dendrocopos major

FAMILY
Picidae – woodpeckers, piculets, wrynecks and sapsuckers

HABITAT
Woods and gardens

SIZE
22–24cm long

DIET
Insects, larvae, seeds, berries and small birds

BREEDS
May–June, one brood

NEST
Hole in tree

EGGS
Four to seven. White

RANGE
Widespread across the UK

COLLECTIVE NOUN
Descent

OLD NAMES
Witwale; spickle pied woodpecker; eeckle; hickwall; woodhacker

The great spotted is the commonest of the four woodpeckers that either inhabit or visit Britain. Other residents are the lesser spotted and the green and they're occasionally joined in summer by the odd wryneck, an ancient brown-barred bird that barely looks like a woodpecker at all. If you've never seen a great spotted woodpecker, you might be surprised at how small they are: roughly the size and shape of a starling. But they're much more boldly coloured – black, white and red all over. Like starlings, they occasionally frequent bird tables and feeders, more so in recent years as more of us decide to feed the birds in our gardens.

The one thing everyone knows about woodpeckers is their mechanical drumming. During the mating season both sexes seek out a suitable sounding board and hammer the life out of it in short bursts with their sharp beaks. What would be headache-inducing to other birds comes naturally to woodpeckers, as the muscles and bones in their skulls have adapted to act as shock absorbers for the brain. They prefer dead wood, but will happily spend hours denting the metal caps of telephone poles if they resonate in the right way.

They live in bored-out holes in a decaying tree, normally in woodland. The young noisily poke their heads out when either parent gets close with a beak full of insects. Adult birds aren't fussy eaters and will plunder seeds, larvae, berries, spiders and pine cones, which they often wedge inside an anvil of bark they construct themselves to break up. To get to grubs they have an extensible tongue that's so long it retracts up and around the skull. True omnivores, they also have a taste for the young of other birds and their long beaks are highly suited to plucking them from the nest – baby blue tits are a favourite snack.

Green woodpecker

Picus viridis

FAMILY
Picidae – woodpeckers, piculets, wrynecks and sapsuckers

HABITAT
Woods, fields and gardens

SIZE
30–33cm long

DIET
Insects, particularly ants

BREEDS
April–May, one brood

NEST
Hole in tree

EGGS
Five to seven. White

RANGE
Scarce but widespread across the UK and Europe, but none in Ireland

COLLECTIVE NOUN
Descent

OLD NAMES
Yaffle; hayhoe; dirt bird; laughing betsy; spick; yappingale; rain pie

Less common than the great spotted variety, green woodpeckers are the largest British woodpecker at over 30cm long, and also the least wood-pecky. Tappers rather than drummers, they are mainly green with a bright crimson crown, black eye-patch and a typically woodpecker-ish chisel of a beak. Jerkily hopping up and down trees in search of grubs, they peck less often than other woodpeckers, and mainly in soft wood as their beak is less robust – although they still bore out holes for nesting when necessary. You're more likely to see a green woodpecker on the ground – their taste for small bugs makes them happy to poke around an ant nest with their extremely long and sticky tongues.

Predominantly larvae eaters – they've been known to try breaking open beehives to get at the grubs – they're also fond of fruit. The young are fed on a regurgitated goo of mashed-up insects by both parents. Green woodpeckers are normally quite grumpy when it comes to mixing with other birds and, outside of breeding season, will often make a solitary hollowed-out home of their own. During courtship they are known to literally run rings around each other up and down trees.

If there's a green woodpecker near, there's a chance you'll hear it before you see it. Its old moniker of 'yaffle' – which those old enough might remember as the name of the professorial woodpecker in *Bagpuss* – refers to its laughing cry, sometimes accompanied by a 'quip quip' alarm noise.

Green woodpeckers are common-ish across continental Europe, but in Britain they're mainly found southward, with few making it to Scotland. Until recently there were none at all in Ireland – it seems ironic that the Emerald Isle isn't blessed with these magnificent, bright green birds.

Nuthatch

Sitta europaea

FAMILY
Sittidae – nuthatches

HABITAT
Broadleaf woodland

SIZE
14cm long

DIET
Insects. Nuts and seeds in winter

BREEDS
April–July, one brood

NEST
Cup built against tree

EGGS
Six to eight. White with reddish brown speckles

RANGE
Widespread in England and Wales, less so in Scotland

COLLECTIVE NOUN
Jar

OLD NAMES
Blue woodpecker; mud-dabber; nut topper; nutjobber; jobbin mud stopper

Nuthatches are small, great tit-sized woodland birds. They have big, almost neckless heads, long bills, grey crowns and backs, a black eye-stripe, white bellies and russet flanks.

Obviously, a physical description of a bird is very helpful for identifying it. But some birds behave so uniquely that even the briefest of distant glimpses can tell you exactly what it is. For example, if you ever see a bird walking headfirst down a tree in the UK, it is an odds-on near-certainty that it's a nuthatch. This agile bird can also run upsidedown along branches. Indeed, so topsy-turvy is its behaviour that it was once believed it even slept upsidedown. It's honestly a shame that it doesn't.

The call of the nuthatch is a high-pitched sharp and repetitive 'siu siu siu', although you may also hear the tapping sound of them trying to crack open nuts they've jammed into crevices. This gives them their unusual name: 'nuthatch' literally means 'nut hacker' in old Middle English. Having said that, they're partial to insects and seeds, too.

Like some other tree-dwelling birds, nuthatches are opportunistic when it comes to choosing their nesting sites. Rather than building their own place, they scan around for a tree crevice, disused woodpecker hole or nestbox to set up home. They then move straight in, narrowing the entrance hole with mud so predators can't enter – a habit that earned them another of their archaic names: 'mud stopper'.

Nuthatches do not migrate. Widespread – but fairly elusive – in England and Wales, they are slowly venturing north into southern Scotland. They'll visit feeders, but they don't like other guests at the dinner table so will probably try to shove off smaller birds.

Hawfinch

Coccothraustes coccothraustes

FAMILY
Fringillidae – true finches

HABITAT
Woods – particularly beech, hornbeam and cherry – parks and orchards

SIZE
18cm long

DIET
Hard seeds such as cherry and plum. Also caterpillars

BREEDS
April–May, one brood

NEST
Twigs and moss, usually in an old tree such as a hornbeam

EGGS
Four to five. White with brown blotches

RANGE
Mainly southern England, common across central Europe

COLLECTIVE NOUN
Company

OLD NAMES
Berry breaker; cobble; pea stripper; cherry finch; cock-hoop

Imagine yourself to be a cherry stone. You're hard. Hard enough to splinter human teeth. Impenetrable. Wait – what? – crack!

The most obvious fact about hawfinches is the incredible power of their bills – enough to split a cherry stone clean in half. A force of 50kg. It's difficult to imagine what that actually means, so here's some context. A hawfinch weighs just 0.05kg. The force it exerts through specially adapted serrations inside its bill is a thousand times its own weight. So, if a hawfinch weighed as much as a 60kg human, its cleaver-like jaw could deploy a pressure of 60 tonnes – about the weight of a house. Ouch.

A berry-breaking bruiser, the hawfinch is Britain's largest finch, though how much it's a 'native' bird is debatable. Up until the mid-19th century, it was mostly confined to continental Europe, where it remains common today. Then over the next century, it advanced across the UK as far as Aberdeenshire, becoming a common sight in orchards and woods. But for largely uncertain reasons, since the 1990s it has suffered a steep decline and numbers are now down to the hundreds. It came, it went, and occasionally – as in 2017 – it still irrupts across the channel when continental crops fail, arriving in winter droves, mainly in the south-east, and vanishing again in spring.

But even during an irruption, you'll be lucky to see a hawfinch. Belying their size and power, they're wary of humans, hiding away at the tops of trees and making barely a sound. Except for the crack of cherry stones.

Treecreeper

Certhia familiaris

FAMILY
Certhiidae – treecreepers

HABITAT
Woods, hedges and gardens

SIZE
12–13cm long

DIET
Insects

BREEDS
April–June, one to two broods

NEST
Behind the bark of a tree

EGGS
Five to six. White with red speckles

RANGE
Fairly common across Britain
and Europe

COLLECTIVE NOUN
Spiral

OLD NAMES
Little woodpecker; cuddy; tree
clipper; tree crawler; bark runner;
eeckle

The treecreeper has been described by some as a small dull-brown bird. But upon that dullness lie beautiful speckled flourishes of white and gold. These pretty birds also have a snowy-white belly and a gently downward-arching beak that allows them to jab into tree bark in search of lurking insects and spiders. They climb in little jumps with their long, curved claws, using their stiff long tail feathers to keep balance.

Treecreepers are distantly related to the wren and around the same size, though with much bigger feet built for climbing. They tend to go about their daily activity in solitude, flitting through woodland, landing at the base of a tree, then climbing in a jagged skipping pattern. Twirling around the trunk until they reach the top, they then fly down to restart the process on the next tree. They work quickly and relentlessly, feeding all day, particularly when daylight is in short supply throughout winter.

Their call is a bold 'tsree!', which often heralds the triumphant discovery of another wooden bug larder. You can spot treecreepers in your back garden, but they much prefer dense woodland, where the interior is warmer and tree bark is less likely to freeze over in wet winters, potentially locking insects away from probing bills. They like mature woods that have deciduous or coniferous trees with furrowed bark to assist with their climbing, but they have also grown fond of the large redwoods brought over from North America.

A loose flap of tree bark can make a cosy treecreeper roost and in colder times up to a dozen have been known to pack themselves into one nook. Their nests are a simple gathering of twigs in crags and tree crevices and the eggs normally hatch in June when caterpillar supply is greatest.

Western jackdaw

Coloeus monedula

FAMILY
Corvidae – crows

HABITAT
Towns, country and coast –
pretty much everywhere

SIZE
32–34cm long

DIET
True omnivores: grain, small
mammals and birds, eggs

BREEDS
April–May, one brood

NEST
Anywhere they can – trees
and chimneys are favourites

EGGS
Four to six. Pale blue
with brown spots

RANGE
Widespread across the
UK and Europe

COLLECTIVE NOUN
Clattering or train

OLD NAMES
Caddaw; corrachan;
john daw; chank; jacky; kay

Being crows – or corvids – jackdaws are supremely intelligent and inquisitive. But unlike others in their family, they use their smarts to spend most days thieving: robbing other birds of their eggs and chicks, picking up useless shiny items and even plucking wool and bugs from unsuspecting sheep's heads.

Just over 30 centimetres long, jackdaws look like a typically black, albeit slightly small, crow from a distance, but have a distinctive grey patch on the nape and neck. Smaller, blunter and twitchier and with a more cackling call than a rook, they can often be seen with their corvid cousins in flocks of thousands. They're found all over Britain and while they may have once preferred open farmland fringed with trees and village buildings, they can now be spotted in small groups in towns and cities.

Jackdaws are largely monogamous, mating for life, but pretty indiscriminate in their nesting habits, sometimes taking over old rook nests. Derelict buildings are also a favourite, but so too are chimneys of occupied homes: get a pair of jackdaws on your roof and your chimney will soon be blocked off by a messy collection of sticks and branches. If cleared by a sweep, the birds will simply set about rebuilding, getting the first parts of their platform back in place in a few minutes.

In the countryside, jackdaws can often be seen clambering and pecking the backs and heads of sheep. It's a mischievously symbiotic relationship where the jackdaw eats the sheep's troublesome ticks, and the bird gets to pull out some wool to line its nest. The delinquency of crows in general and jackdaws in particular was a favourite metaphor of Aesop, who used the bird in several of his fables of human fallibility.

Magpie

Pica pica

FAMILY
Corvidae – crows

HABITAT
Woods, heaths and gardens

SIZE
40–50cm long

DIET
Omnivorous: seeds, birds, insects, carrion

BREEDS
April–May, one brood

NEST
Dome in a tree or bush

EGGS
Five to eight. Pale blue and olive

RANGE
Widespread across the UK, more recently extending its range to the north of Scotland

COLLECTIVE NOUN
Charm

OLD NAMES
Chatternag; Cornish pheasant; maggoty-pie; mock-a-pie; nanny; tell-pie

Whether it's one for sorrow, two for joy, or warily wishing them a good morning, our relationship with magpies has always been a mix of reverence, mistrust and a little hatred. Even putting the mysticism to one side, there's still a great deal of disquiet when magpies turn up in the garden. They're renowned for taking small birds, but the truth is they only do so in the summer when they have their own young to feed. They mainly eat grubs, and recent studies have shown they have negligible impact on songbird numbers. Magpies' true function is tidying the carrion that litters the countryside, and you'll often see them near roads, waiting for the next unfortunate pheasant or deer to meet its end.

Magpies are corvids, or crows, and, at half-a-metre or so long, sit somewhere between a rook and a jackdaw in size. A lot of that is made up by a long, wedge-shaped glossy black tail, iridescent with greens and purples, of which science has yet to figure out the definite purpose. They tend to walk slowly on the ground, but can break into a canter of frantic hopping. While not the most agile in the air, their long tails can help them glide from one high vantage perch to another.

Magpies are supremely intelligent and it has recently been suggested that they may be among the smartest animals on the planet, up there with humans, the great apes, dolphins and whales. Although their brains are relatively small, the neurons are tightly packed and they are among the few animals that recognise their own reflection. They also have a habit of hiding food and a notorious love of shiny objects. Or do they? We used to think magpies stole jewellery because they were dazzled by it, but science now seems to believe it scares them, although not so much that they lose their curiosity to investigate.

Dipper

Cinclus cinclus

FAMILY
Cincliae – dippers

HABITAT
Fast streams and rivers,
usually at altitude

SIZE
18cm long

DIET
Insects, worms and small fish

BREEDS
February–April, two broods

NEST
Ball of moss in bankside hole

EGGS
Four to six. Glossy white

RANGE
Widespread across Britain,
apart from the south-east

COLLECTIVE NOUN
Ladle

OLD NAMES
Best docker; water craw; ess cock;
willy fisher; water blackbird

The dipper is a dumpy small bird with a dark brown body, a white chin and breast and a short stubby tail. It is adapted like no other to feed beneath the surface of fast-running water: it's watertight and has natural nose plugs, a translucent third eyelid that draws across the eye to act like swimming goggles, and a large preening gland on its bottom that allows it to wax its own feathers. Its haemoglobin-rich blood can store high concentrations of oxygen, which means it can hold its breath under water longer than other birds.

A dipper's bones are solid, which in shallower water allows it to fully submerge and move along the riverbed in search of insect larvae and fish eggs like an agile avian deep-sea diver. Dippers are also blessed with large unwebbed feet that help them grip beneath the surface and have small but powerful paddle-like wings that enable them to fly underwater (what we'd call 'swimming'). Their flight above water is low and straight.

While you may be forgiven for thinking the dipper owes its name to its proclivity for dipping in streams, the moniker in fact describes its habit of bobbing up and down on stone perches before sliding or walking into the water. In the 18th century it was known as the water ouzel – a Medieval English name referring to pretty much any black bird that today survives in the form of the ring ouzel, or mountain blackbird.

Dippers have three ways of communicating: high-pitched calls, a blend of bobs and dips, and a Morse code-style technique that involves blinking their white eyelids. These delightful little birds can be found all year round on fast-running upland streams throughout northern Britain.

Pheasant

Phasianus colchicus

FAMILY
Phasianidae – pheasants and partridges

HABITAT
Countryside – woods and fields

SIZE
Females 50–65cm long,
males 75–90cm long

DIET
Seeds, berries and grasses

BREEDS
April–June, one brood

NEST
Hollow on the ground,
hidden in undergrowth

EGGS
Seven to 15. Olive

RANGE
Introduced all across
Europe from Asia

COLLECTIVE NOUN
Bouquet

OLD NAMES
Comet; cock-up; ffesant

A kaleidoscopic mix of colour, sound and stupidity, pheasants are a gamebird, non-native to Britain but introduced so long ago that they've become an iconic sight in the UK countryside. The males are almost a metre long, around half of which is the tail, with a mottled copper-coloured body, metallic green head, red wattles around the eyes and a distinctive white collar that gives them their North American name of 'ring-necked pheasant'. The females are smaller and less ostentatious, patchy and brown, deliberately discreet to help them hide when nesting on the ground. Nesting pheasants can be easily missed – as I discovered. For three weeks one sat on its nest by the side of our house. Until one day it was gone. All that was left were the shells of freshly hatched eggs – the chicks had already wandered off with their mother.

Originally from Asia, the first British pheasants were brought from the Caspian Sea before 1066, possibly by the Romans, but extirpated by the 17th century. The first ring-necked pheasants came from China in the late 18th century, and they've been kept and raised by gamekeepers ever since. Birds that have escaped the gun have gone on to breed freely across Britain, highly suited to our countryside and climate. They nest under hedges and on the fringes of woodland, coming out in large numbers to feed on farmland, gobbling up seeds, fruits, insects and earthworms.

Given how much human intervention has shaped the pheasant, I'm never sure whether their stupidity is natural or deliberately bred-in. When alarmed they take off almost vertically, wings whirring and clapping, accompanied by a noisy 'kark-kark' call just in case they went unnoticed. When not flying they're running, normally towards danger, never heading for the safety of the verge when taking on a car is an option.

Grey partridge

Perdix perdix

FAMILY
Phasianidae – pheasants and partridges

HABITAT
Countryside and fields

SIZE
30cm long

DIET
Seeds, grasses and insects

BREEDS
April–May, one brood

NEST
Hollow on the ground

EGGS
Ten to 20. Off white

RANGE
Widespread across Europe, but rare at northern and southern extremities

COLLECTIVE NOUN
Covey

OLD NAMES
Girgirick; grey bird; paitrick; stumpey; grigear

There are two breeds of partridge resident in Britain. The grey or common partridge is native to Britain and found in small groups across the country. The other is the red-legged variety –sometimes referred to as the French partridge – which was imported from Europe during the 18th century as a gamebird, but has since naturalised.

Common partridges are rotund and heavy 30 centimetre-long balls of orange, chestnut and grey standing on stumpy legs that help them duck down in fields if alarmed. Arable farmland, particularly wheat fields, is their preferred habitat but anywhere with some rough and patchy cover for them to hide will do and they're not fussy about moorland and heaths. Like many gamebirds – they belong to the same family as pheasants – they're not fond of flying long distances, preferring to dash about on the ground and only taking to the air when danger, either perceived or real, comes calling. When relaxed, they'll stroll around with their heads tucked down, becoming feathery balls with legs. But if they feel the need to make a run for it, they stretch their necks up and scurry away, heads pointing to the sky.

You'll probably encounter partridges in two contexts. One is in the countryside, and if you see one, there are sure to be more around, either youngsters hanging around with their parents or in small groups known as 'coveys'. The other is when singing 'The 12 Days of Christmas'. However, as ground-loving birds, the chance of seeing one in an actual pear tree is virtually zero.

Birds of Wilder Places

Harsh weather, rough terrain, ungodly hours and spending all day travelling for a fleeting glimpse – seeing the birds of our wilder places requires that extra bit of effort. Some are rarer and vagrant species; others are abundant but simply choose to live in the places we don't. Among them are many iconic birds of the British Isles, and most people go their whole lives without witnessing them.

Golden eagle

Aquila chrysaetos

FAMILY
Accipitridae – raptors

HABITAT
Woodland, heaths and fields

SIZE
75–90cm long

DIET
Small mammals, birds and carrion

BREEDS
March–August, one brood

NEST
Cliff edge, occasionally trees

EGGS
One to three. White with
brown blotches

RANGE
Mainly northern and
western Scotland

COLLECTIVE NOUN
Aerie

OLD NAMES
Jove's bird; mountain eagle; erne

A golden eagle's eyes are so large and tightly squeezed into its head that it's unable to move them around within the sockets. Their eyes are approximately the same size as our own – each weighing more than its brain – but theirs are deeper, letting in more light, and packing in more receptor cones and rods. That gives it dual focus of both the central and peripheral fields, meaning it can see a rabbit from two miles away, but it also has UV vision, enabling it to trace the urine trails of its prey.

To see a golden eagle, you need to go to the wild places and look up. Long ago, you could have spotted one soaring over many of the barren mountains of Britain, but today they have largely retreated to the Highlands and south-west of Scotland, rarely the Lake District. Numbers have slowly dwindled as habitats have changed and food sources become scarcer, but also because of the large area an eagle needs to cover to find sufficient food. You can occasionally sight birds in odd places. Once diligently raised by their parents, youngsters are chased off their patch and forced to seek fresh hunting grounds elsewhere. For that reason, there are rare instances of juvenile golden eagles being spotted on the fringes of the Highlands in places such as Moray.

Using their two-metre wingspans, eagles attain high altitude and can generally be seen amid the clouds above remote open upland. This allows them to optimise their magnificent field of vision and utilise one of their other assets, speed. Golden eagles can dive at up to 150mph with an agility you would associate more with peregrine falcons. Their predatory arsenal is completed by a very large set of talons, which they use to catch and kill, and a long sharp beak for rending flesh.

Ring ouzel

Turdus torquatus

FAMILY
Turdidae – thrushes

HABITAT
Mountains and moorland

SIZE
23–25cm long

DIET
Insects, berries and worms

BREEDS
April–mid-July, one to two broods

NEST
Small cup on the ground

EGGS
Four to five. Blue with
brown markings

RANGE
Migrant to the mountainous areas
of the north and west of Britain

COLLECTIVE NOUN
Hermitage

OLD NAMES
Amsel; collared blackie; fell blackie;
Michaelmas blackbird; mountain
blackbird; rock starling

Not all birds are black and not all black birds are blackbirds, even if they very much look like them. The ring ouzel is a case in point. It may closely resemble a blackbird but it has a distinctive white bib around the top of the breast, most prominent in adult males. Further inspection also reveals silver-lined black feathers, which give the bird a scaled appearance.

Ring ouzels are migratory, breeding in the spring and summer in western, central and Scandinavian Europe and spending the winter in Mediterranean Europe and North Africa. In Britain they're chiefly found in the uplands of the north, although they may be seen in coastal regions during their migratory passages in spring and autumn. 'Ouzel' is an old English word for blackbird and the species was once known as the mountain blackbird. If you're lucky enough to see one – and you'll need to be in the mountains of mainland Britain to stand the best chance – enjoy viewing it from a safe distance: ring ouzels are very shy.

Ring ouzel numbers have mysteriously declined in Britain and Ireland since the 20th century. Studies have recently centred on the very low survival rates of first-year birds, which could be attributed to either shifts in agricultural practices, climate change, increased competition from other species, migratory issues or a combination of all of the above.

Omnivorous, they feed on insects, earthworms and perhaps the odd small rodent or lizard in spring and summer. In autumn and winter their diet turns to fruit and berries, especially juniper berries, so much so that an old Scottish name for the bird is 'chat of the juniper'. Dubbing it a 'gin thrush' might be going a bit far, however – ring ouzels have yet to master the art of distillery.

Chough

Pyrrhocorax pyrrhocorax

FAMILY
Corvidae – crows

HABITAT
Sea cliffs and coastal moorland

SIZE
35–40cm long

DIET
Insects, seeds and worms

BREEDS
April–May, one brood

NEST
Crevices, cliffs and ledges

EGGS
Three to four. Pale green-brown with brown and grey spots

RANGE
Western coasts of the UK, predominantly Wales

COLLECTIVE NOUN
Chattering or clattering

OLD NAMES
Chauk daw; sea-crow; red-billed jackdaw; killigrew; Cornish daw; hermit crow

'Ker-chuff, ker-chuff' is the call that gives the chough its odd name. These peculiar birds are glossy black corvids, roughly the size of jackdaws, but more slender and with long bright-red beaks and legs. In Britain they are lovers of high coastal places and were once known as sea-crows, nesting on cliff faces and occasionally steep quarries. The British red-billed varieties don't fly so high as their Alpine relatives, which have straighter yellow bills and are found up in Europe's snowcapped mountains.

Hugely acrobatic, choughs use thermals to soar high above the cliffs before folding their ragged wings and plunging, sometimes rolling on to their backs as they do so. When not in flight they can be found in rocky crevices, either nesting in gaps in the cliff face or notches in a cave wall, or poking around with their long beaks for insects, spiders and small lizards. Choughs are monogamous, pairing for life, and once settled will often stay at the same nest. Once common across Cornwall – so much so that they appear on the Cornish coat of arms – choughs died out on the peninsular in the early 1970s. The last female passed away in the late sixties, but her male partner stayed on to keep patrolling as a solitary widower for a few more years.

Dripping in Arthurian legend – it's said King Arthur didn't die but transformed into a chough – they are, sadly and like many birds, in decline across Britain and now mainly found in Wales. Choughs require pasture: their food derives from grassland kept short by livestock and, as animals have been moved away from the coast for easier management, their numbers have sunk. Their co-dependency with grazing livestock extends to the fact that, much like jackdaws, they will pick ticks and wool from sheep for food and to line their rocky nests.

Lapwing

Vanellus vanellus

FAMILY
Charadriidae – plovers

HABITAT
Farmland, especially wet
meadows, marshes and mud flats

SIZE
28–31cm long

DIET
Invertebrates, seeds and grasses

BREEDS
March–June, one brood

NEST
The female selects one scrape
from several the male has made.
Lined with plant material

EGGS
Four. Light to dark brown
with darker markings

RANGE
Most of the UK and central Europe

COLLECTIVE NOUN
Deceit

OLD NAMES
Flapjack; horny pie; flopwing;
peewit; bastard plover

A bird of beauty, deception and desolate places, the lapwing was once commonplace across all Britain. Meeting in winter in dark congregations over barren fields – no tree cover, no place for a crow to watch on – it's on sharp spring evenings during the annual search for a mate when you'll find lapwings leaping and wheeling in a black mass. Given the acrobatic display, carried on oversized wings, you might imagine their name to be a corruption of 'leap wing'. But 'lap' is an ancient Frisian allusion to their signature crest. Or maybe to the lapping sound of pulsating wings. Or possibly just leaping… The 'wing' part must be more straightforward, though, right? Not really. It likely comes from the old English 'wince', meaning the rise and fall of a winch, so nothing to do with wings at all.

All that's just the start of the deception. Offering flashes of white in its dark plumage, the lapwing is a simple black-and-white bird. Or is it? Closer inspection reveals iridescent purple and green, orange, browns, blacks, contradictory camouflage. Approach one and it will appear injured, leading you away, wailing with a broken wing. But this is just a distraction display as it deliberately steers you from its young or eggs as they rest in no nest to speak of, making do with a hollow in the soil.

Peesweep. Peewit. Teuchit. Old onomatopoeic names, prized by poets. But 'bastard plover'? Loathing lapwings was routine in times of religious persecution when their shrill screams were blamed for betraying those who fled for refuge in the crops. Later, their eggs became a delicacy, until the Lapwing Act of 1926 prohibited their consumption. Thankfully, we're now more in thrall to this confusing, tricksy bird, whose groups, it's no surprise to learn, we dub a 'deceit'.

Wheatear

Oenanthe oenanthe

FAMILY
Muscicapidae – Old World
flycatchers

HABITAT
Heathlands and grasslands

SIZE
14–15cm long

DIET
Insects

BREEDS
April–May, one to two broods

NEST
Cup wedge between rocks or
in abandoned rabbit burrows

EGGS
Five to six. Pale blue

RANGE
Summer visitor to the UK.
Winters in sub-Saharan Africa

COLLECTIVE NOUN
Swatting

OLD NAMES
Ailing; barley bird; fallow finch;
clod-hopper; whishie

There's something truly remarkable about the wheatear. The birds that we see summering in the UK have come from sub-Saharan Africa. Nothing to be sniffed at, but nothing too special either – swallows, ospreys, warblers and a host of other birds do that, too. What makes wheatears so special is that every spring they take flight from central Africa to points across the globe, returning there each autumn. So, rather than just Britain or northern Europe, they reach Alaska, Canada and northern Asia, crossing deserts, mountain ranges, oceans and ice caps to get there. Those Alaskan migrants average a round trip of 20,000 miles.

But what is a wheatear and what makes it so wheaty? Much like robins, they used to be members of the thrush family. But they've recently been kicking birds out of that particular nest and wheatears have found a new home among the flycatchers. Across Europe, they tend to live in mountains, but in the UK they can often be found nesting in alternative crevices: gaps in stone walls, beneath discarded planks, under railway sleepers and embankments and even in abandoned rabbit burrows on the stony ground they favour for hunting insects.

As for the wheaty part? Well, wheatears are wheaty in colour and I've always associated them with stony areas near fields of wheat. But the uncomfortable truth is that the name has nothing to do with wheat at all, but instead refers to its white rump. Yes, every time you see a wheatear you're really looking at a little 'white-arse'.

Bearded reedling

Panurus biarmicus

FAMILY
Panuridae – bearded reedlings

HABITAT
Reedbeds

SIZE
12–13cm long

DIET
Invertebrates in summer,
seeds in autumn/winter

BREEDS
April–August, two to three broods

NEST
Deep cup in reeds

EGGS
Four to five. Creamy white

RANGE
Sparse, mainly in the south and
east, Lancashire has the biggest
UK population. They also live in the
reedbeds at the mouth of the River
Tay in Perth and Kinross, Scotland

COLLECTIVE NOUN
Banditry

OLD NAMES
Bearded pinnock; beardmanica;
least butcher bird

Over time many birds get a change of name. I often think that some of the older titles were that bit more charming, more beautifully descriptive, or simply funnier, and it's a shame we've got so serious and scientific about what we call things. Most old names are archaic throwbacks, originating either from local dialect, Old/Middle English or foreign tongues, but changes continue to this day and can even happen in our lifetimes. When I was a kid in the 1970s there was a bird called the bearded tit, but it no longer exists. Or rather, the bird itself does, but it's now known as the 'bearded reedling'.

Science is to blame. Back in the 18th century when Carl Linnaeus set about classifying the natural world, he placed the reedling in the *Paridae* family – tits, chickadees and titmice. Later scientists discovered it wasn't related to the tits, so decided to move it into the parrotbill family, *Sylviidae*. More recently, it was thought to be related to the lark family, the *Alaudidae*. And now? DNA evidence shows that it isn't really closely related to anything else at all, and so it sits in a family all of its own, *Panuridae*.

The reedling is a small long-tailed passerine with a blueish head and orange body. Adult males having a distinctive black moustache. Unlike its tit not-cousins, it is extremely unlikely to visit gardens as it lives exclusively in reed banks, especially those near the coast. The British population is limited to a few colonies, numbering a couple of thousand birds sparsely spread across the country. In spring/summer they dine upon aphids, changing their diet to reed seeds in the winter, while making a distinctive 'pinging' call all year long.

Kingfisher

Alcedo atthis

FAMILY
Coraciiformes – kingfishers, bee-eaters, rollers, motmots and todies

HABITAT
Freshwater rivers and lakes

SIZE
15–16cm long

DIET
Small fish

BREEDS
April–June, two broods

NEST
Hole in bank

EGGS
Six to seven. White

RANGE
Scarce but widespread across Britain

COLLECTIVE NOUN
Crown or realm

OLD NAMES
Salop fisher; halcyon; sea blue bird of March

Across the world there are over 100 species of kingfisher, but the British variety, the common kingfisher, is the only one found widely across Europe. You get a hint of this stumpy bird's exotic, tropical nature by its extravagant colouring – dazzling cobalt from the top of the head to tail, the underparts a warm chestnut orange, with flashes of a white collar and a long black spear of a bill. It's certainly an unusual bird for northern Europe. They and their other kingfisher cousins belong to a group of misfits known as *Coraciiformes*, which is made up of other bits-and-bobs birds such as rollers, bee-eaters and motmots, all totally different, none quite fitting elsewhere.

Despite their colouring, kingfishers are surprisingly hard to spot. As fishers, they can usually be found near freshwater. Perching on a favourite branch above a stream, river or lake, they use special adaptations in their eyes to reduce the glare of the water and compensate for refraction, making them extremely accurate when plunging on to small fish below the surface. In flight they're a whirring flash of iridescent colour, but can also hover over the water – although you've more chance of seeing one silently water watching or beating a freshly caught fish against its perch.

They nest in holes built into steep banks by slow-moving water, excavated by the birds to a depth of sometimes 60 centimetres or more. Courtship takes place in the autumn, but the pair keep their own space until spring when they merge territories. To find a mate, a male kingfisher has to prove his speed, stamina and ability to fish. The female allows herself to be chased by the male, who catches a succession of minnows, presenting them as fishy gifts to his prospective partner.

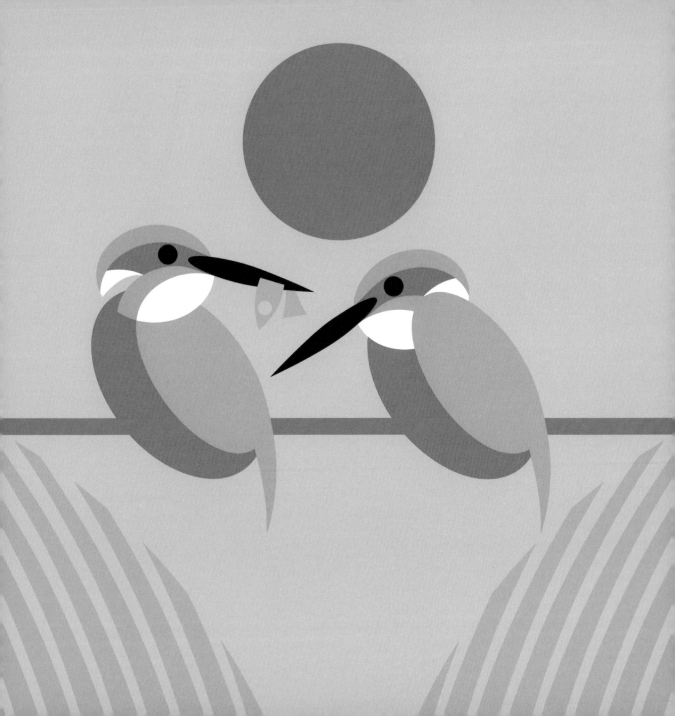

Grey wagtail

Motacilla cinerea

FAMILY
Motacillidae – wagtails and pipits

HABITAT
Shallow rivers and streams, particularly in west – and northern areas; sewage farms and other wetland areas in winter

SIZE
17–20cm long

DIET
Insects, molluscs and crustaceans

BREEDS
March–July, three or more broods

NEST
Located in a hole, made of mostly plant material and lined with hair and feathers

EGGS
Three to six. Light brown with some streaked markings

RANGE
Occurs over much of the UK and south-west and central Europe

COLLECTIVE NOUN
Volery

OLD NAMES
Oatseed bird; winter wagtail; yellow handstir; barley bird

Wagtail by name, wag tail by nature, but which way does a wagtail's tail wag? Up and down or side to side? I used to think the answer was obvious, but there's nothing obvious about Britain's twitchiest of birds. You'll probably know the pied variety – a small black-and-white bird that's either scurrying around car parks or frantically twitching its tail, but never, ever, just being still. Twitch. Twitch. Twitch.

We often use 'pied' to describe black-and-white birds: the lapwing is also known as the horny pie, although it's more cresty than horny, and absolutely not monochrome. Pied wagtails are almost uniquely British and when I lived in Sussex I associated them with winter – when the northern birds would pile in to escape the cold at higher latitudes. In Europe they have a cousin, the white wagtail, which isn't really white, just a bit greyer than our pieds. Sometimes in winter they get a splash of yellow… Then there's the yellow wagtail, which is yellow. And the grey wagtail, which is also yellow. Enough to make anyone twitch.

What's the difference? If you're by running water, and you spot a yellow bird with a bobbing flight catching small insects, it'll likely be a grey.

But up and down or side to side? Let's leave it to John Clare, Romantic poet of the British countryside and son of a farm labourer, for the answer: "*Little trotty wagtail he went in the rain, And tittering tottering sideways he near got straight again*". Clear? Nope. Twitch.

Bohemian waxwing

Bombycilla garrulus

FAMILY
Bombycillidae – waxwings

HABITAT
Breeds in conifer forests, migrating to the UK in winter

SIZE
18cm long

DIET
Leaves, berries and fruit and insects during the breeding season

BREEDS
June–July, one brood

NEST
Twigs in conifers

EGGS
Four to six. Blueish grey

RANGE
Northern and eastern Europe, irrupting across the west in winter

COLLECTIVE NOUN
Museum

OLD NAMES
Bohemian chatterer; silk tail; wandering waxwing; Bohemian jay

Fortunately for mistle thrushes and other berry-loving British birds, waxwing irruptions do not happen every year. It is only when fruit supplies are low on the continent that waxwings leap over to Britain in great numbers. But in the years they do, they arrive here in their hundreds or thousands, much to the delight of local birdwatchers.

Waxwings get their name from the markings on their wing tips, which look like glossy red sealing wax. The size of starlings, they are not hard to spot, all fluffy crests, black-lined eyes and grey-pink plumage, with flashes of gold, white and red. Their scientific name of *Bombycilla* refers to their silky feathers, and fits with their ornate looks but also their blustering, noisy and bombastic character. They sit within a clade of birds that DNA analysis has shown to have a common ancestor and also includes the Japanese and cedar waxwings, plus certain chats, flycatchers and whistlers.

Waxwings feed insects to their young in summer, but otherwise live off the fruits of a variety of trees and bushes. They are especially fond of white rowan berries. Nomadic by nature, they move from one fruity bush or tree to another until supplies are utterly spent, at which point they may cross the sea, much to the dismay of local birdlife. In Britain, they normally irrupt across the north and east first, from December onwards, having started a journey in crop-failed Finland and Russia but, as area by area is exhausted of fruit, spread across the country. Like all winter migratory birds, when the larder is spent and the weather turns back towards spring, they scatter back across the North Sea. Whether we see them the following year is a lottery largely drawn in the Baltic.

Common crane

Grus grus

FAMILY
Gruidae – cranes

HABITAT
Open ground near water

SIZE
100cm long

DIET
Roots, grain, fruits and seeds.
They will also eat insects
during the breeding season

BREEDS
May–June, one brood

NEST
Mound on ground

EGGS
Two. Pale, spotted red or brown

RANGE
Sparse across western Europe

COLLECTIVE NOUN
Siege

OLD NAMES
Garan; grew; piper

When my nephew was small he was a boy of few words. However, while being driven around in the back of my car, he was often given to pointing excitedly at the sky and chanting "Crane! Crane! Crane!". I have to admit I found his obsession with construction machinery rather irritating, given that it only sought to remind me of the lack of large trumpeting birds in my life…

Until around the end of the 16th century, the common crane was a resident British bird, but then disappeared from our shores. These days, tiny populations have returned to East Anglia and in recent years the Wildfowl and Wetland Trust has set up breeding programmes in Somerset, releasing almost 100 birds over five years. Common by name, less so by nature, cranes may be sighted at any time of year, but they are very rare in Britain. Although our country's tallest bird, these grey, heron-like creatures with a ludicrously loud honking call are both easily disturbed and flighty.

Common cranes pair for life and, during the mating season, couples will try to find their own private spaces to build a flat nest to raise their chicks. Their annual mating display involves dancing, jumping around with their wings lifted, while bellowing ear-piercing calls.

Boggy woodland and swamps are their preferred habitat. But cranes are opportunistic and omnivorous in their feeding and could be found anywhere close to water. The majority of the breeding population is in Russia and eastern Europe. However, once they have bred and finished their moult, they will gather in vast numbers and migrate south to warmer climes in Africa, the Middle East and parts of Asia, where they are venerated as symbols of youth, happiness and longevity.

Peregrine falcon

Falco peregrinus

FAMILY
Falconidae – falcons and caracaras

HABITAT
Anywhere with cliffs – quarries, even towns and cities

SIZE
40–50cm long

DIET
Birds of all sizes

BREEDS
March–June, one brood

NEST
Scattered on high ledge

EGGS
Two to four. Cream with red/brown markings

RANGE
Found across Europe

COLLECTIVE NOUN
Bazaar

OLD NAMES
Pigeon hawk; saker; tassel gentle; gentile falcon; blue sleeves

A great many British birds fear the peregrine falcon, and so they should. The sight of a feathered death missile screaming down at 200mph is enough to send any avian gathering scattering in a blind panic. This partly explains why birds such as knots and starlings murmurate, as it enables them to confuse and evade this lightning-fast raptor.

The peregrine falcon is a powerful bird of prey that adds small mammals and reptiles to a hit-list mainly made up of small- to medium-sized birds – in the Americas they are sometimes known as duck-hawks. Indeed, anywhere you find large flocks of birds, such as moors, marshland or cliffs, could attract the attention of the wandering peregrine.

Peregrines are highly manoeuvrable and can swoop down to give chase to their prey, or use a stoop technique in which they fold their wings and drop on their victims from the sky. Unfortunately, the species' keen hunting instincts mean it has suffered from persecution in Britain. In the 1950s and '60s, peregrine numbers were greatly affected by agricultural pesticides. Such chemicals are no longer used today, but peregrine deaths by poisoning or gunshot are still reported.

Peregrines nest on ledges, particularly at cliffs, building a shallow depression known as a scrape. When observing a pair of peregrines you might sometimes think you're looking at an adult and one of its young. However, they're likely to be an adult pair as the female is much bigger than the male. Whatever their size, though, if you see mallard mayhem at a local estuary, a peregrine falcon is likely to blame.

Hen harrier

Circus cyaneus

FAMILY
Accipitridae – hawks, eagles and kites

HABITAT
Moorland, grassland, marshes

SIZE
40–50cm long

DIET
Small birds and mammals

BREEDS
April–June, one brood

NEST
Twigs on ground

EGGS
Four to six. Pale blue to white

RANGE
Once widespread, now endangered across the UK

COLLECTIVE NOUN
Swarm

OLD NAMES
Blue gled; dove-coloured falcon; katabella; ring tail; furze kite

Hen harriers are beautiful birds of open moors and heathlands, with long wings and tails and a languidly elegant flight. They fly low to the ground, owl-like faces boosting their hearing, so they can ambush small birds and mammals. Like other harriers, they are sexually dimorphic: the smaller males are blue-grey, while the larger females, as well as immatures, are mostly brown with a distinctive ringtail. This difference in colouring is largely down to the fact that the female is the main parent: nesting on the ground, leaving chicks vulnerable to badgers, crows, foxes and other predators, its drabber colour gives it a degree of camouflage. Males, on the other hand, often take many mates over a season, their ghostly grey hue advertising their dandyish presence.

Hen harriers from the continent may boost numbers in winter. At that time of year, hen harriers sometimes communally roost in numbers and even share space with other raptors. Globally, their conservation listing is 'least concern', but it's a rare resident in the UK and has a conservation red listing here.

Since the 19th century and the growth of grouse drives, hen harriers have been persecuted in the UK because their predation of grouse chicks is thought to have a negative effect on grouse yield for the shooting season. At the beginning of the 20th century, there were no hen harriers at all on mainland Britain. They were reintroduced in the 1940s, but since the 1990s have declined sharply. Hen harriers are among the birds protected under the Wildlife and Countryside Act of 1981, but illegal shooting, trapping and nest spoiling still goes on today. There are various campaigns to help protect them, all hoping to succeed in maintaining these grey ghosts and ringtails on our shores.

Nightjar

Caprimulgus europaeus

FAMILY
Caprimulgidae – nightjars

HABITAT
Heaths and woodland clearings

SIZE
27cm long

DIET
Moths and other insects

BREEDS
May–July, one to two broods

NEST
Scrape on the ground

EGGS
Two. Cream blotched with black

RANGE
Sparse European population, migrates to Africa for winter

COLLECTIVE NOUN
Kettle

OLD NAMES
Big razor grinder; churr owl; corpse bird; gabble ratchet; moth hunter

Imagine a summer meadow at dusk. The woodcock have roded, the rabbits have congregated at their burrow's edge and, as the sun descends, an eerie churring of nightjars rises. In this way, one of the briefest love affairs in a birdwatcher's life may begin…

Nightjars arrive in Britain in spring and migrate back to Africa in late summer. That unmistakable churring noise is the call of the male as it sits in the shade of a tree. If you ever hear it, keep watching the trees and wait for the call to stop, as this is when it will take flight to prey on small night-dwelling insects and moths. Nightjars are crepuscular – active at dawn and dusk. During the day, they lie still on the ground or in the branches of trees – some have been known to lie in a rigid state of torpor for days – which can make them very difficult to spot, as their mottled skin helps them blend into their surroundings.

Nightjars are blessed with soft feathers that enable them to fly quietly, while the males also have white flashes on their feather tips that they use in wing-clapping displays. They hunt by sight, which is why their activity is limited to dawn and dusk, and both sexes have wide gapes and bristles around their mouths to expand their reach. Nightjars get their Latin name, which means 'goatmilker', from the myth that they used to suckle goats and stop them from producing milk. However, these days these secretive summer visitors are content to dine on moths in the summer twilight.

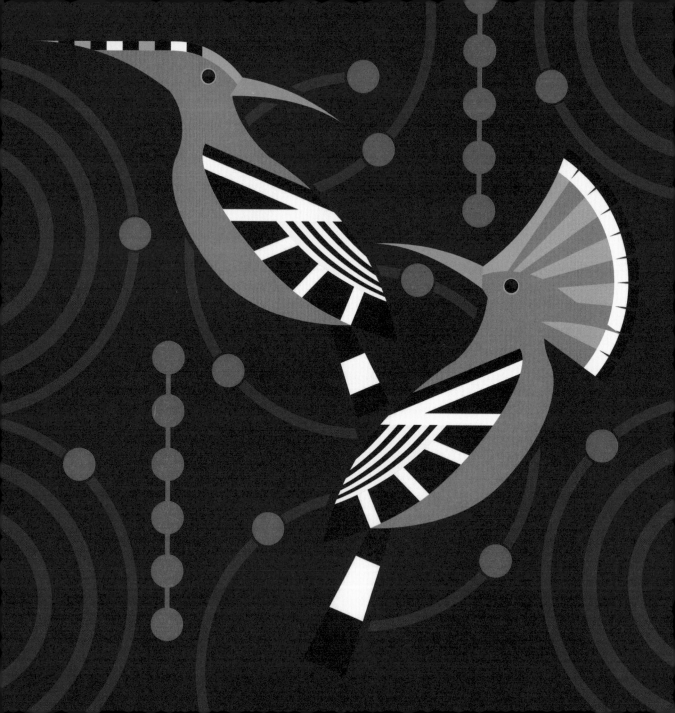

Hoopoe

Upupa epops

FAMILY
Upupidae – hoopoes

HABITAT
Woods, heaths and fields

SIZE
27–30cm long

DIET
Insects

BREEDS
April–June, one brood

NEST
Stinky hollow in a tree or rocks

EGGS
Five to eight, though the clutch sizes tend to be bigger further north and can contain up to 12 eggs. Pale blue

RANGE
Summer visitor to Europe, some – very few – making their way across the Channel

COLLECTIVE NOUN
Cry

OLD NAMES
Hoop; houp; dung bird; child of Solomon

The Eurasian hoopoe is a bird with a crazy crest, and an equally crazy name, that flies like a butterfly and has a particularly stinky nest. Around the size of a blackbird, they are an odd browny-orange colour, with distinctive black-and-white bars on the back and wings and a long, black, gently curving bill. They are mainly found in continental Europe, but each year a handful fly over the Channel to the south-east and East Anglia, with fewer still blown off course all the way to Scotland.

The crest is usually down, but is raised when they become excited and is a possible explanation for the name: its French title, *huppe*, means crested. Another is that it comes from its call, a low 'hoop-hoop-hoop' heard only during courtship. Maximum hoopiness is supplied by its Latin moniker – *Upupa epops* – the most pleasing scientific name to say out loud.

In flight, a hoopoe looks like a giant butterfly or moth, with stripy, rounded wings that almost touch on each wingbeat. They feed mainly on the ground, picking up larvae, but their long curved bill, adapted to probing the soil, is attached to special muscles in the skull and mandible that allow it to open up underground with huge force.

For such a beautifully unusual bird, a hoopoe's habits are disgusting. They happily search for food in dung heaps, pressing their faces deep down into the muck to find small grubs – hence their old name of 'dung bird'. But they also take their indifference to poo home with them. Their nests, usually a hole in a tree, are renowned for being ridiculously smelly. A hoopoe never cleans out its home, letting it fill up with faeces, while females secrete a foul-smelling odour to ward off predators. When not stinking the place out they can often be seen resting on the ground, wings outstretched, crest up, head back, soaking up the sun.

Coast & Wetlands

You have to be committed to watch birds by the water. But once you've struggled past the wind, rain, mud, cold and gulls, it's worth it. This is where you'll experience some of the most specialised birds, lovers of extreme conditions, with some of the most outrageous of evolutionary quirks. These are birds that are adept on land, sea and air.

Atlantic puffin

Fratercula arctica

FAMILY
Alcidae – auks

HABITAT
Coastal cliffs and offshore waters, only coming ashore during breeding

SIZE
28–30cm long

DIET
Small fish and squid

BREEDS
May–June, one brood

NEST
Cliff-top burrow

EGGS
One, white

RANGE
Mainly Scotland. Largest populations are further north in Iceland and the Faroes

COLLECTIVE NOUN
Circus

OLD NAMES
Parrot-billed willy; bulker; sea parrot; cockandy

The Atlantic puffin – the clown of the sea – is among the most recognisable and best-loved birds in the UK. But, as so often with clowns, it has a tinge of melancholy to its tale.

Let's start with what a puffin is: an auk, a family of upright black-and-white sea birds noted for being a bit clumsy on land but able to 'fly' underwater – puffins can descend 60 metres to dig up their favourite meal of sand eels from the sea floor. Auks spend more time at sea than anywhere else and in that respect they're like penguins, although the two are totally unrelated and, unlike penguins, auks have the added advantage of being able to fly.

Puffins are possibly the squattest of auks: tiny multi-coloured dumplings, with carrot-coloured legs and splashes of red and yellow around the bill. They make land once a year, raising a single chick inside a burrow. Lacking their parents' coloured bills, the youngsters are known as pufflings, an undeniably endearing name for an undeniably endearing bird. Which makes the following fact all the harder to swallow: in Iceland and the Faroe Islands, the young and eggs of these comical, waddling, industrious and largely monogamous birds are a delicacy.

The clue to this is in the name, although not their own. *Puffinus* is the Latin word for the shearwater, a completely different bird that also nests in burrows and lays a single egg. Puffin, an Anglo-Norman word meaning 'fatling', was applied to the salted carcasses of cliff-dwelling birds traded around Scotland, Ireland and all points north. Somewhere along the way that name settled on our puffin, sadly marking it out as food.

Great northern diver

Gavia immer

FAMILY
Gaviidae – divers

HABITAT
Freshwater and at sea
(rarely on land)

SIZE
70–80cm long

DIET
Fish and amphibians

BREEDS
May–September, one brood

NEST
Scrape close to the water's edge

EGGS
Two. Pale olive with black spots

RANGE
Breeds in Iceland, Greenland and
Canada, winters mostly around
the colder coastlines of northern
Europe

COLLECTIVE NOUN
Asylum

OLD NAMES
Amber goose; cobble; naak; great
doucker; greatest speckled diver

The great northern diver is the largest of the divers – or loons if you're in North America – roughly the size of a large duck or small goose. Lovers of cold places, they spend their summers breeding in Greenland, Iceland, Svalbard, Canada and Alaska but, when the conditions get too chilly even for them, they head south and pitch up along the Atlantic coastlines of northern Europe and both sides of the USA. Just over 2,000 arrive around Britain from August onwards, but they're a bird very much associated with winter and the north. You'll occasionally be lucky enough to see them taking shelter from rough weather in Scottish harbours; otherwise, you'll need a good pair of binoculars, as they spend most of their time off the coast.

As the name suggests, they're especially adapted for diving. Most birds have bones that are hollowed out to make them lighter and aid flight, but divers – like penguins – have heavier, solid bones to make them less buoyant. With a thick layer of fat to insulate against the cold, a streamlined dagger of a bill, oily feathers so densely packed that they don't look feathery at all, and legs stuck at the rear and acting like an outboard motor, they can dive down 60 metres foraging for fish. They only come ashore during breeding, and their legs have adapted so well to life at sea that they're almost useless on land and unable to support their bodyweight: great northern divers have to push themselves along the ground on their fish-filled bellies.

Gannet

Morus bassanus

FAMILY
Sulidae – gannets and boobies

HABITAT
Sea, cliffside nests

SIZE
85–100cm long

DIET
Fish

BREEDS
April–June, one brood

NEST
Seaweed on cliffs

EGGS
One, white

RANGE
North Atlantic coastlines; largest colonies in the world are in the UK

COLLECTIVE NOUN
Gannetry

OLD NAMES
Bass goose; solan goose; gant; guga; spectacled goose

With an impressive 1.8-metre wingspan, the northern gannet is the pointiest, whitest and largest bird of the British coastline. They're not entirely white: they have a yellow stain around the head and some black at the wing tips. But you're likely to miss those features seeing them at a distance, glistening high in the sky as the sun reflects off their oily feathers as they fold their pointy wings and plunge towards the water.

The largest gannet colonies on the planet can be found on the deserted islands of Scotland. Up to 75,000 birds at a time make their nests on rocky outcrops such as Bass Rock and St Kilda, and the UK is home to close to two-thirds of the world's population. But you don't need to head out on a boat to see gannets: there is a large mainland colony at Troup Head in Aberdeenshire, where you can get up close to them for as long as you can put up with the head wagging, bill clashing and pungent fishy smell.

Like their relatives the boobies, they're renowned for their insatiable appetites – which is why 'gannet' has come to mean a greedy-guts. They use their wings and air sacs built into their bodies like scuba gear to swim down as far as 25 metres to catch fish. They're not the best at taking off, though, and need high cliffs to launch from. However, once airborne they can go on 200-mile round trips, working their way up to heights of over 60 metres, bright blue eyes peering down in search of fish shoals.

When they spot one, they make like a missile: folding everything tightly together and smashing into the surface at 60mph, leaving a visible plume of water in their wake. Enough to break most other birds, this behaviour is only possible thanks to a number of evolutionary adaptations: strong necks, nostrils inside the bill to stop water ingress, protective membranes over the eyes and a super-streamlined shape.

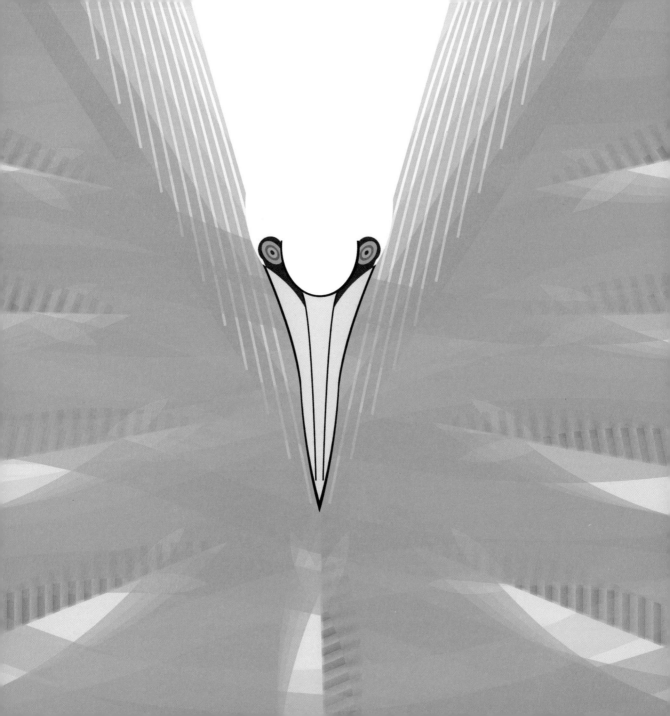

Cormorant

Phalacrocorax carbo

FAMILY
Phalacrocoracidae – cormorants
and shags

HABITAT
Sea, estuaries, lakes…
anywhere there is water

SIZE
85–90cm long

DIET
Fish

BREEDS
April–June, one brood

NEST
Seaweed mound or sticks
when they nest in trees

EGGS
Three to four. Light blue

RANGE
Widespread across the
waterways of Europe

COLLECTIVE NOUN
Gulp

OLD NAMES
Brongie; beacon bird; ralphie;
shagga; cotton heap

The cormorant (or great cormorant to give it its full name) is one of the two British members of the family *Phalacrocoracidae* – the other being its closely related cousin, the shag. To my eye they've always looked very similar – largish, long-necked, almost goose-like black with a petrol sheen of purples, bronzes and greens, and long but not-too-pointed bills – and I still struggle to tell them apart. Quick rule of thumb: the shag is smaller and has a crest, which British cormorants lack.

Although generally found near the sea, cormorants aren't exclusively coastal birds and can be spotted in freshwater areas, such as the lochs and rivers of Scotland, sometimes even nesting in trees during breeding season. The birds that do stick to the coastline never really venture far from land, but they're not bothered by bad weather and it's not unusual to see cormorants flying low over the water's surface in even the stormiest of conditions. Once back on land, they'll stand bolt upright on a rock, often unfurling their wings to dry off.

Cormorants skimming over the sea are not an unusual sight, but they're not overly adapted to flight. For birds that swim, dive and fly, there is always a trade-off: shorter wings are better for diving, longer ones for flying long distance. Cormorants push the envelope of efficiency by having short wings that allow them to swim effectively in choppy waters, but at the same time make them poor and cumbersome in the air. It may not look it, but their flight is hugely uneconomical and uses up enough energy to always keep them close to shore, whether inland or by the sea.

Common eider

Somateria mollissima

FAMILY
Anatidae – ducks, geese and swans

HABITAT
Sea and estuaries

SIZE
55–60cm long

DIET
Molluscs and crustaceans

BREEDS
May–June, one brood

NEST
Hollow close to water

EGGS
Four to six. Off green

RANGE
Seen all year round, migratory birds arrive in the UK in large numbers from Iceland over winter

COLLECTIVE NOUN
Quilt

OLD NAMES
Banganner; Cuthbert duck; Cuddy duck; dunter; coo-doo; dusky duck

The eider is a spectacular sea-duck that frequents the coastlines of northern Britain in reasonably large groups all year round. The males – or drakes – are more striking than the females: mainly white with a black crown and splashes of green and yellowy-pink. As is typical with ducks, the females are less conspicuous, with mottled warm-brown plumage that helps keep them camouflaged on the rocky beaches where they nest. While they do breed in Britain, their numbers swell during the colder months when migrants flee the harsher Icelandic conditions. Look out to sea during a Scottish winter and you'll see large groups of them bobbing about in the rough weather, occasionally diving for the shellfish and crabs that they swallow whole. Occasionally, a solitary king eider – a close, but more brilliantly coloured and hardier relative – will have attached itself to a migrating group and made an unnecessary trip to the UK.

Eiders are sociable ducks and when nesting in large colonies – anything up to 15,000 strong – will happily help out neighbours and relatives by crèching each others' young. The ducklings are raised in a shallow nest softened by downy feathers from the female bird. These feathers also provide good insulation for the youngsters – important when you make your home in the worst the North Atlantic has to offer – and have been used by humans for centuries. The down left behind after the birds have fledged can be harvested without causing them direct harm. However, once-popular eiderdown duvets and jackets have now largely been replaced by those stuffed with more efficient human-made fibres.

Sandwich tern

Thalasseus sandvicensis

FAMILY
Laridae – gulls, terns and skimmers

HABITAT
Low-lying coastal beaches

SIZE
35–40cm long

DIET
Marine fish

BREEDS
May–June, one brood

NEST
Shallow scrape

EGGS
One or two. Creamy white with black/brown/grey speckles

RANGE
South-east and north-west of Britain and north-east

COLLECTIVE NOUN
Hogey

OLD NAMES
Surf-tern; screecher; crocker-kip; boatswain

How and why birds get their names is always interesting. Sometimes they're pretty simple descriptions of colour (as in blackbird or blue tit). Sometimes they describe a noticeable feature (great crested grebe) or a noticeable behaviour (song thrush). Occasionally, they're named after a naturalist (Montagu's harrier) or aristocrat (Lady Amherst's pheasant). And often they relate to a habitat, whether that's general (Atlantic puffin) or specific (tree sparrow). But what to make of a bird given the forename 'sandwich'?

Sandwich terns are longer and visibly heavier than their cousins the – suitably named – Arctic, common and roseate terns. Terns can be difficult to tell apart from a distance, but as well as its size, the sandwich tern also stands out because of its crested head, solid black cap and yellow tip on the end of its snappy knife of a bill. Its diet is predominantly a mix of sand eels, small fish, worms and crustaceans.

Mainly coastal birds, terns on the wing can be mistaken for gulls at a distance. But they're sharper all over, with wing tips, elbows and tails as pointy as their bills and, unlike gulls, will plunge-dive to catch their prey. Hovering at a distance above the water, they make use of eyes specially adapted to cut through haze and water to smash into shoals of fish just below the surface.

But do they eat sandwiches? Unfortunately not. Or probably not – prawny ones could possibly tempt them. The truth is the name derives from Sandwich, Kent, where the ornithologist John Latham first described them back in the 18th century. Pity.

Eurasian oystercatcher

Haematopus ostralegus

FAMILY
Haematopodidae – oystercatchers

HABITAT
Marshes, estuaries, fields
(increasingly urban areas)

SIZE
40–45cm long

DIET
Molluscs and earthworms

BREEDS
April–July, one brood

NEST
A scrape in sand or among pebbles

EGGS
Two to three. Cream with
brown spots

RANGE
Particularly northern Britain,
also Scandinavia and Iceland

COLLECTIVE NOUN
Parcel

OLD NAMES
Bride's page; sea-magpie; olive;
oyster plover; mere pie; sea pie

Just how do you catch an oyster? They can't really run away and if you're a British oystercatcher, chances are you've never even encountered a real-life oyster. The name comes from its American cousins, which are mainly from the Deep South and enjoy a hearty gumbo diet. In the old days in Britain, we used to call them 'sea pies' (in reference to their black-and-white markings rather than an actual pie), but it's a pity we passed on the opportunity to legitimately have a British bird called a winklepicker, cocklecruncher or musselmuncher.

You'll usually hear an oystercatcher before you see it. Its distinctive piping call alerts you to its presence as it flies on rapid wing beats low across the shore or fields, foraging for cockles, mussels, worms, crustaceans and insects. They use their long bills to probe into rock pools on the shore line and the soft earth of inland meadows, but – as I've seen in northern Scotland – they can get confused in urban environments. There's something truly tragic about seeing an oystercatcher trying to break through the tarmac of a local authority car park to get at the non-existent cockles beneath.

The longest-lived bird recorded was just over 40 years old. Ringed as a chick in 1970 it was last caught in the same place, by a ringer, on The Wash in 2010. Incredibly it was never seen away from the site in the intervening years.

Pied avocet

Recurvirostra avosetta

FAMILY
Recurvirostridae – avocets and stilts

HABITAT
Marshes and estuaries

SIZE
40–45cm long

DIET
Insects, crustaceans, worms

BREEDS
April–May, one brood

NEST
Bare scrape, or hollow

EGGS
Four. Pale brown with black spots

RANGE
Temperate coastal areas
across Europe, except for
northern Scandinavia

COLLECTIVE NOUN
Colony

OLD NAMES
Barker; black-and-white flighter;
crooked bill; shoeing horn; scooper

With stunning white plumage, patterned black across the crown and nape, spindly blueish legs and a bill unique among British birds, pied avocets are unmistakable and difficult not to spot if they're around. You'll find them scattered across the UK on mudflats, brackish lagoons and estuaries, feeding in shallow water. They're easy to recognise from a distance by their dazzling whiteness, but it's their topsy-turvy bill that sets them apart.

Or should that be a beak? The terms are pretty much interchangeable and even nit-picking twitchers don't seem to have any hard-and-fast rules about which is which – other than that ducks have bills and garden birds have beaks (mainly). Either could be used in the case of the avocet, but the difference is that, unlike almost every other bird, its one points the wonky way up. Long and slender, and shaped like a scimitar, an avocet's bill is used for skimming over water, catching insects, molluscs, worms and fish spawn, head waggling from side to side as it moves. In deeper water, avocets are happy to upend themselves tail to the sky, dabbling like ducks. When excited or disturbed they also go in for a bit of frantic head-bobbing, but once calmer they'll tuck one leg up like a flamingo, rest their slender bills on their chests and drop off to sleep.

For over a hundred years, no avocets bred in Britain. They were wiped out in the 1840s – their eggs were taken for pies, their feathers for fishing flies – but they began appearing again in East Anglia just after the Second World War. By the 1970s there were around 150 pairs aided by conservation and the work of the RSPB – which adopted the avocet as its logo. They've now spread as far afield as Scotland, breeding there again in 2018 for the first time in over a century and a half.

Black-winged stilt

Himantopus himantopus

FAMILY
Recurvirostridae – avocets and stilts

HABITAT
Shallow pools and coastal lagoons

SIZE
33–36cm long

DIET
Insects

BREEDS
April–June, one brood

NEST
Bare scrape, or hollow

EGGS
Three to four. Pale olive
with black spots

RANGE
Mainly Spain, Portugal and France
but rare vagrant to northern Europe

COLLECTIVE NOUN
Generic

OLD NAMES
Long shanks; stilt plover;
long legs; long-legged plover

Stilt by name, stilty by nature. For a wader, the black-winged stilt is a long-legged giant. Tall among British wading birds, ours is illustrated alongside the stint, among the shortest. Obviously these things are relative. Don't go expecting a bird the size of a giraffe as even the spindliest of waders is only around 33–36cm long. But with its almost ridiculously long pink legs – which make up around 60 per cent of its total length – bright red eye, pointy black-and-white wings and pointier still jet-black bill, the stilt stands head and shoulders above its wading neighbours.

Related to avocets, stilts are infrequent visitors to the UK, but pop up all over the world – there are stilts as far afield as Hawaii. Ours, however, tend to fly in from Africa in the spring. They struggle to breed in Britain, with only a handful of instances over the past 30 years or so, but in 2017 a record number managed it. Thirteen chicks fledged across the country, with seven of them occurring at the RSPB's Cliffe Pools site in Kent where years of conservation work has created an ideal freshwater/brackish marshland habitat.

Those gangly legs were made for wading, allowing black-winged stilts to squelch out further than their cousins in search of food. They mainly pick up insects from the water's surface or drifting vegetation but will – with some difficulty – pick up food from the ground. Graceful in the air, stilts fly with everything outstretched: neck long, their legs together and held out horizontally from the back. But such elegance comes at a price: too top heavy to be effective walkers, they waddle about on land with wings aloft to avoid toppling over.

Spoonbill

Platalea leucorodia

FAMILY
Threskiornithidae – ibises and spoonbills

HABITAT
Marshes and estuaries

SIZE
80cm long

DIET
Insects, fish, crustaceans

BREEDS
April–May, one brood

NEST
Large platform on islands or in reeds or trees

EGGS
Four. Off white, reddish markings

RANGE
Scarce in the UK, more common in mainland Europe. UK birds have generally migrated from the Netherlands

COLLECTIVE NOUN
Canteen

OLD NAMES
Shovelard; banjo bill; popeler; sholarde

There's something strange and exotic about a spoonbill. Standing slightly shorter than a heron at just under a metre tall, and frequenting similar haunts, spoonbills are tall, sparklingly white birds, elegant until you get to the bill. Where a heron has a dagger, spoonbills possess a clumsy-looking broad flat spade of a beak that widens at the tip to produce the spatulate form its name suggests. They're among a number of birds that have recently started making their way back into Britain after a breeding absence of centuries, and I still find them outrageously odd and excitingly misplaced – an unfamiliar ibis among the 'little brown jobs' we normally think of as British birds.

Wading out on marshes and shallow water, they sweep their bills from side to side latching on to anything they encounter. Special nerve-endings make the bill highly sensitive to touch and, if they happen upon something edible, they'll swallow it. While they seem to prefer small fish, insects, worms and crustaceans, they are truly omnivorous and are just as happy spooning out vegetable matter from the estuary gloop.

Sociable by nature, they can congregate in groups of up to 100, building nests on platforms in reed banks, small islands or even in the branches of trees. In Britain you're more likely to see them in smaller clusters or as pairs, which have likely wandered over from established breeding grounds in the Netherlands. Their large, unwieldy and specialised bills may be useful for feeding, but they also make them reliant on each other for keeping clean: mutual preening is a distinctive spoonbill activity.

Great crested grebe

Podiceps cristatus

FAMILY
Podicipedidae – grebes

HABITAT
Lakes, reservoirs, gravel pits and coastal areas in winter

SIZE
46–51cm long

DIET
Fish, crustaceans, molluscs, tadpoles, frogs and insects

BREEDS
April–August, one brood

NEST
A mound of floating vegetation fixed to adjacent plants

EGGS
Three to four. White

RANGE
Most of the UK except for northern Scotland, but found over much of west, central and eastern Europe

COLLECTIVE NOUN
Water dance

OLD NAMES
Arsfoot; cargoose; rolling pin; ash-coloured swan loon; greater horned doucker

Being the crestiest and largest of the European grebes, these seem to have been well named. But what their moniker doesn't tell you is a) quite how spectacular they are, b) that, like all grebes, they're related to flamingoes, and c) they used to be called arsfoots.

The great crested grebe was the first bird on my must-see list. It was my gateway drug to birdwatching, if you will – the one that got me excited even before I'd seen it in the wild. But, exotic-looking as they are, they're not actually that difficult to track down – these days, at least. But it wasn't so long ago that their feathers were so prized by milliners that they were down to their last 30 pairs in the UK. Admittedly, you won't see a great crested grebe in your garden, but head to any of Britain's many nature reserves situated around reservoirs or lakes and you stand a good chance. Visit Rutland Water and your chances of seeing that dagger of a bill in action climb higher still.

The best thing about great crested grebes is their courtship dance. It's been called balletic, but only if you like a few wet weeds with your *pas de deux*. Fanning out their elaborate ruffs, a courting pair synchronise swims and bob their heads, climaxing with a frankly improbable rearing up out of the water and then presenting each other with… a bundle of dank pond grass. Romantic? Yes, if you're a grebe.

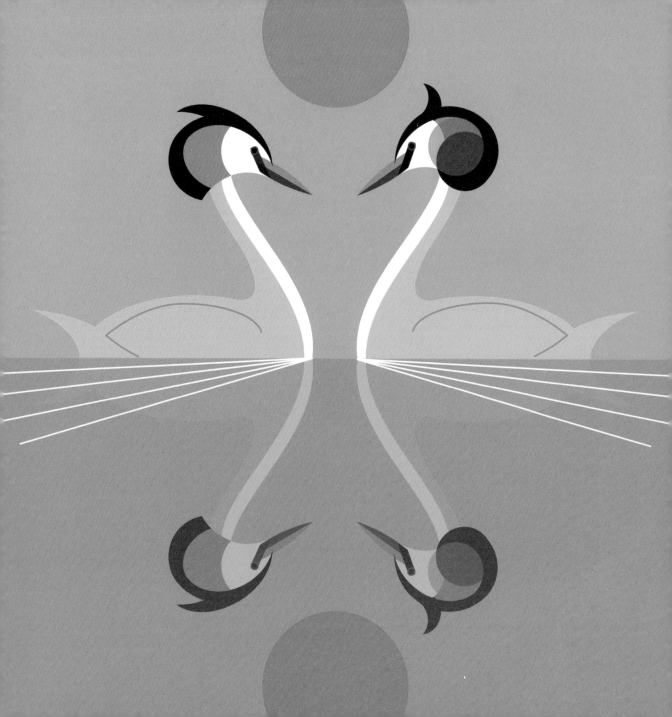

Grey heron

Ardea cinerea

FAMILY
Ardeidae – herons and egrets

HABITAT
Mainly freshwater but can
be seen on coastal margins

SIZE
90–100cm long

DIET
Fish, amphibians, small mammals

BREEDS
February until May or June,
one brood

NEST
Large platform high in trees

EGGS
Three to five. Greenish blue

RANGE
All over the UK,
wherever there is water

COLLECTIVE NOUN
Siege

OLD NAMES
Butter bump; craigie heron; frankie;
long-necky; lung-necked yern

The grey heron is one of Britain's biggest birds, standing a metre tall and a remarkable sight in flight. They appear even larger in the air, head drawn up into an arc on an extensive neck, legs straight out from the back, languidly flapping past on long, lazy wingbeats. Found anywhere there is water, you can encounter herons on coasts, rivers and estuaries across the UK, usually stood upright, still and silent as they wait for an unfortunate and unsuspecting fish, eel, frog, vole or small bird to wander too close and be swallowed head first in one gulp.

For a bird that likes to have its own patch of river, lake or even ditch, they are surprisingly gregarious and congregate in breeding colonies known as heronries. These are usually high up in trees and the largest colonies, such as at Cleeve in Somerset, contain up to 50 nests. They return to the same nests year after year, gradually refurbishing them from small clumps of twigs and branches to huge spiky saucers. While most herons nest in trees, in the absence of cover they will also nest on the ground in reed beds and, certainly in the north of Scotland, the sight of 20 herons stood stock still at dawn or dusk on the banks of an estuary is not unusual. But these aren't always heronries – they also like to hang out together in separate groups known as 'sieges'.

Grey herons are members of the *Ardeidae* family and can be found in various guises across the globe. Until recently, just two members made their home in Britain – the heron and its distant, and ridiculously elusive, cousin the bittern – but they've recently been joined by an influx of egrets, making the most of the opportunities offered by a combination of our improving conservation and land management, and climate change.

Northern shoveler

Spatula clypeata

FAMILY
Anatidae – ducks, geese and swans

HABITAT
Marshes, estuaries and lakes

SIZE
45–53cm long

DIET
Crustaceans, water plants
and seeds

BREEDS
April–May, one brood

NEST
Hollow near water's edge

EGGS
Eight to 12. Plain buff colour

RANGE
Seen all year round, but migrate
both north and south. In the UK
more common in the south

COLLECTIVE NOUN
Chain gang

OLD NAMES
Blue-winged shovel bill;
maiden duck; kertlutock;
broadbill; sheldrake

The shoveler is a muck-loving duck, slightly smaller than a mallard, with a similar bright-green head but a completely different bill. Much like the spoonbill, and unlike most birds, its beak is spatulate – broad at the tip and thinner where it meets the body. It's also its most noticeable feature: from a distance you should pick up the bottle-green head, white chest and ruddy flanks of the drake (like most ducks the female is a camouflaged brown) but, close up or through binoculars, it's all about the bill.

The bill must be disproportionately heavy, as shovelers almost always swim with their heads carried low, and is the result of an extreme adaptation to a system of feeding employed by many ducks. They like marshes and lakes, preferring to be close enough to the water's edge that the shallow and muddy bottom is within reach. Snapping up vegetation and small animals on the water's surface, they use fine-toothed-comb-like plates between the bills like a sieve to trap small pieces of food as they siphon water. This action of skimming water through the bill to extract food is known as dabbling, and many ducks do it, though few so efficiently as the shoveler.

Shovelers can be seen across Britain all year long, more so in the south than the north. If you're lucky to see them locally in both summer and winter, they're almost certainly not the same individuals, however. The birds that breed in Britain generally migrate south to the warmer climes of Spain and France in winter. But as one lot goes, another arrives to take over the pitch: the hardier northern breeders of Russia and Scandinavia. Come spring they'll do it in reverse, the birds briefly overlapping for a festival of shovelling.

Shelduck

Tadorna tadorna

FAMILY
Anatidae – ducks, geese and swans

HABITAT
Sandy estuaries

SIZE
60–65cm long

DIET
Algae, snails and grasses

BREEDS
April–June, one brood

NEST
Hole in the ground

EGGS
Eight to ten. White

RANGE
Coastal around western Europe

COLLECTIVE NOUN
Doading

OLD NAMES
Banganner; bargoose; beer gander;
St George's duck; skeeling goose

There's a bit of abductive reasoning called the duck test that goes, "If it looks like a duck, swims like a duck and quacks like a duck, then it's probably a duck." It's a bit lazy, but you'd think that when applied to an actual duck, there'd be some logic to it. Unfortunately, life ain't that simple, even when the 'duck' in question has 'duck' in its name.

The shelduck stands out on mudflats, estuaries and coastlines as a rather large bird with splendid plumage, a loud honking call and, although at home swimming in saline waters, is more likely to be spotted standing by the water's edge. Most female ducks tend to be less colourful, so they blend into their surroundings when nesting. But female shelducks have the same splendid colouring as the males, which means they have to hide when nesting, usually in a vacant hole not too far away from water.

Once the young have hatched and are reasonably self-sufficient, they form into crèches watched over by a handful of non-breeding carers. Meanwhile, the majority of adults migrate to mass moulting grounds, gathering in their thousands to shed and replace their plumage, leaving them flightless for weeks. Over 100,000 shelducks from across northern Europe congregate on the Wadden Sea in Germany, but there's also a smaller gathering at Bridgwater Bay on the Bristol Channel.

The missing 'l' in shelduck looks like a typo, but neither 'shel' nor 'duck' mean what you might think. '*Shel*' is an old Dutch word meaning variegated, and has nothing to do with shellfish. What's more, the shelduck isn't really a duck at all. Instead it's related to the Egyptian goose. Both sit in the *Tadorninae* subfamily, an evolutionary middle ground somewhere between geese and ducks. So, if it looks like a duck, swims like a duck… it's not necessarily a duck.

Water rail

Rallus aquaticus

FAMILY
Rallidae – rails

HABITAT
Reed banks

SIZE
20–27cm long

DIET
Molluscs, insects, small mammals

BREEDS
Late March–August, two broods

NEST
Small dish just above water

EGGS
Six to 11. Off white
with reddish spots

RANGE
Widespread but elusive

COLLECTIVE NOUN
Reel

OLD NAMES
Bibcock; jack-runner; oar-cock;
skitty cock; rat-hen

Water rails are so shy and retiring that you're unlikely to ever see one. That's a pity as they're an amazing bird, slightly smaller than a moorhen, blue across the chest, streaky brown and black on the back, and with a long red bill unique among British rails and crakes. However, if you're ever near swampy sedge or reed banks and hear a grunting and squealing that sounds like a pig, you'll know there's a water rail 'sharming' nearby.

Like its coot and moorhen cousins, the water rail has extraordinarily large feet, made for spreading its weight over floating vegetation as it creeps through reeds. But, unlike those, it is not a fond swimmer, rarely taking to the water, and if forced to do so will stay neurotically close to cover. Outside of sharming sessions, water rails are masters of stealth, managing to remain virtually silent as they carefully pick their way through tall and rustly vegetation, barely making a sound. If disturbed while nesting – and just about anything is enough to make a water rail nervous – they have been known to carry away their young or eggs in their beaks and set up home in a new nest.

Rails are laterally compressed. That's a fancy way of saying they're a bit skinny. It helps to be thin when you spend half your life creeping between reeds and the other half petrified of making the slightest noise. Some have suggested that the phrase 'thin as a rail' refers to these almost two-dimensional birds. Unfortunately, that's not the case: the water rail gets its name from the Old French '*raale*', a death rattle or scraping noise, reminiscent of its call. Secretive and neurotic, yes, but this elusive bird can still rail against the world like an angry hog.

Next steps

Appetite whetted? Immersing yourself in the world of birds is among the most rewarding things you can do for yourself, your children, your friends and the environment. But where to begin? Britain is blessed with some amazing nature reserves and a selection of bird organisations devoted to, and doing great work for, our native birdlife. Some are national, but there's almost undoubtedly a local bird club or Wildlife Trust near you. Many of them arrange regular talks and guided walks. Here are a few addresses to get you started:

Royal Society for the Protection of Birds (RSPB) *rspb.org.uk*

British Trust for Ornithology (BTO) *bto.org*

Wildfowl & Wetlands Trust *wwt.org.uk*

The Wildlife Trusts *wildlifetrusts.org*

Natural England *naturalengland.org.uk*

Natural Resources Wales *naturalresourceswales.gov.uk*

Scottish Natural Heritage *snh.org.uk*

Scottish Ornithologists' Club *the-soc.org.uk*

Sussex Ornithological Society *sos.org.uk*

Index

About the author

Distilling the natural world into something simple and beautiful, Stuart Cox is the founder of Scottish brand I Like Birds, which produces bird-themed designs with universal appeal for use on stationery, textiles, mugs and all manner of other bird-based bits and bobs.

Acknowledgements

I function predominantly as a designer, so never get the chance to thank people in print. The short version is this: if you know me and have helped along the way, thank you. Truly, without such an amazing group of friends, family, work colleagues, design colleagues, social media followers, licensees and licensing agents, my life wouldn't be half as good as it is. But as I've got the opportunity, there are some people I should single out. It could be the only chance I ever get. In no particular order:

Alison, my partner, the other half of 'I Like Birds', without whom I would probably have descended into lunacy. She mops my brow, makes my tea, tells me what's good or bad or just a bit 'meh'. Most of all she makes me happy.

Stephen, my brother and main conspirator when it comes to bird facts. Thank you for being so encouraging, for stepping into the breach when I lost my way, for being such a key part of this book and for being so amazingly supportive in all I do. Most of all, thank you for being my brother (not that you had a choice).

My departed family: mother, father and brother. And my second family of Lyn, Chris, Stephanie, Kim, Phil, Alfie and Nollie. Thank you for everything. No, really.

Cat and Ria, my not-so-evil pair of adopted daughters. Sorta. Anyway, you make me laugh. Sometimes it's at you.

My extended family of uncles, aunts and cousins, for sharing your love of nature, for making life fun, and just for being there when I need you.

Ian. Thanks for being such a great mate and exceptional wingman.

To all the amazing people at Hardie Grant Publishing, who make work not seem like work at all, but in particular to Melanie for taking a punt on us in the first place, Emily for just 'getting' me and the sometimes odd ways I like things done, and to Zena and Harriet for being such kind, thoughtful and helpful editors. Always gracious, always productive, you're a fantastic team to feel part of.

Nikki, Gaby, Paul, Jackie, Nigel, Kevin, Dave, Joe, James, Ged, Karen, Jack, Jon, Emma, Gill, Dan, Ben, Margaret, Nicola, Another James and Afzal – our 'I Like Birds' partners in bird-based nonsense. I'm proud to call each of you a friend.

To Simon. Not sure why I'm thanking him. He just asked me to do it. He's like a marketing munchkin. He's also my mate. And to his mum, Tracey.

To Mel, Jess and Richard at JELC. Mainly to Jane Evans, my licensing agent and co-collaborator in all things 'I Like Birds'. Without her wisdom, kindness, drive, support and all-round amazingness, I wouldn't be doing this now.

To many others. But, most of all, to Alison x.

PUBLISHING DIRECTOR
Sarah Lavelle

COMMISSIONING EDITOR
Zena Alkayat, Harriet Butt

SENIOR DESIGNER
Emily Lapworth

ILLUSTRATOR
Stuart Cox

PRODUCTION
Vincent Smith, Katie Jarvis

———————————————

Published in 2019 by Quadrille,
an imprint of Hardie Grant

Quadrille
52–54 Southwark Street
London SE1 1UN
quadrille.com

Design and layout © Quadrille 2019
Text and illustrations © Stuart Cox 2019

Cataloguing in Publication Data:
a catalogue record for this book is
available from the British Library.

ISBN 978 1 78713 417 1
Printed in China

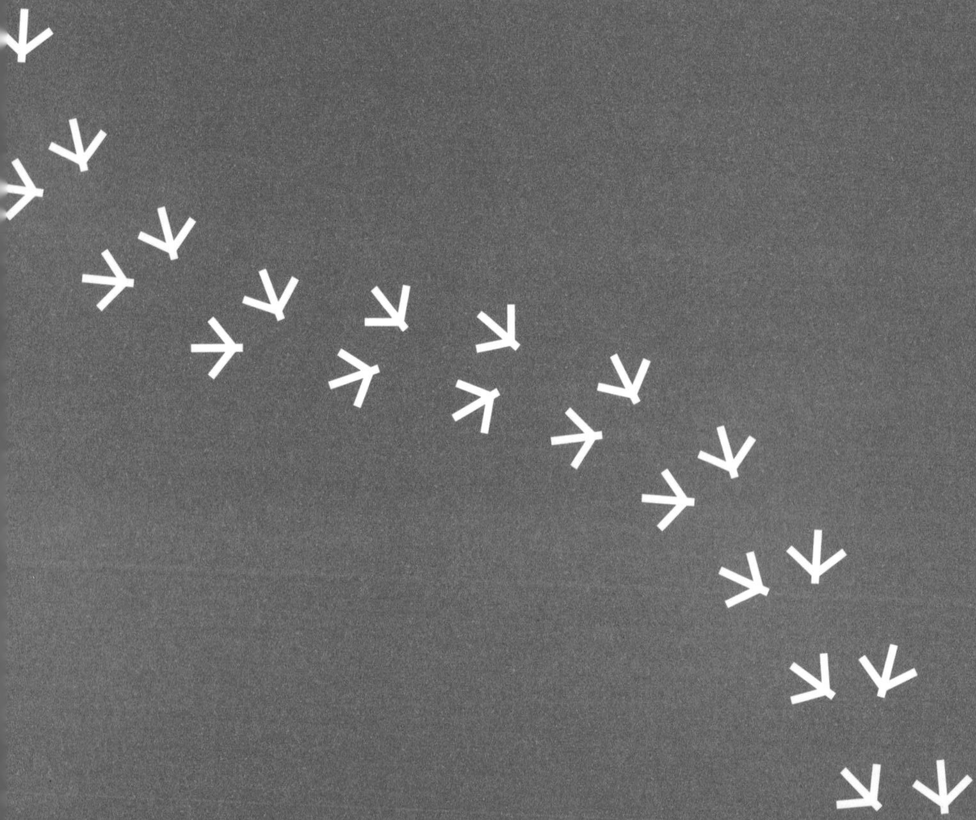

I
LIKE
BIRDS